FIRST FIELDWORK
The Misadventures of an Anthropologist

Barbara Gallatin Anderson
Southern Methodist University

WAVELAND

PRESS, INC.
Prospect Heights, Illinois

For information about this book, write or call:
Waveland Press, Inc.
P.O. Box 400
Prospect Heights, Illinois 60070
(847) 634-0081

Cover: Illustration by Mary Vernon

For Andrea, the intrepid

Contents

Prologue

The chapters that follow bear little resemblance to conventional ethnographic accounts of village life. This acknowledgment warrants explanation, inasmuch anthropologists are not given to sportive approaches to first fieldwork—an experience with sober ramifications professionally. It may be helpful for the reader to learn the chain of events which led to this book's particular character.

First fieldwork launches neophyte anthropologists on the commendable and lifelong goal of advancing scientific knowledge along a very specific frontier. In reporting appropriately in print on their joint progress toward this goal, anthropologists keep one another in business, university departments and various centers of research flourish, and the science itself is rightfully perpetuated.

Actually, I was in the process of writing a defensibly scholarly book on fieldwork when I had a telephone call from Mrs. Slade a real estate agent who was marketing my late father's home.

She had a buyer for it.

"There's still quite a bit of stuff I haven't gotten out of the house," I said.

"Can you get to it?" she asked. "They aren't quibbling on price, but they want possession by the fifteenth of next month."

"I'll get on it," I promised.

It was good news. The bad news was that I had now to address myself to a chore I'd been avoiding—going through an accumulation of possessions I had no heart for exploring. And so, on the following afternoon, I collected boxes from the neighborhood liquor store and began sorting the salvageable things from the things to be thrown away in my father's home. It was late in the day when I finally got to a locked cabinet whose key was in a lacquered box on his desk. And there, in a collection of shoe boxes, I found every letter I had written to him over the years from field sites around the world.

Letters in frail airmail envelopes bore stamps from locations that ranged from India to Costa Rica, from Morocco to Japan. From first fieldwork in Denmark to my trip to China completed a month before his death. Stored in the most orderly fashion, chronologically by country of origin, each envelope was dated across its face in his careful script.

Once among the most active of men, my father had suffered a crippling heart attack shortly after my mother's death. Out of my deep affection for him—and guilt over my long absences—I had written him intimately and at length of my life as an anthropologist.

I moved the boxes to my office and closed the house. During the next week I read the letters, every one of them: a record of more than two decades of field activity. Stories of it all: the personal as well as professional dimensions of life as an ethnologist. Week by week, the stuff of fieldwork.

I came away from it amazed, the memory of worlds recreated by the letters vivid in my mind. People and places long forgotten suddenly sprang to life. How could it be? I asked myself. How could I have forgotten it all? I could see again the landscapes through which I had moved. The houses in which I had lived. Smell the wallpaper paste in an ancient French cottage, feel the weight of India's monsoon heat, recall the spices that clung to the clothes of my Moroccan guide. All were newly familiar.

And above all, engulfing and fresh and riotous was the memory of first fieldwork—of life in a Danish fishing village. The tiny, windswept island that enclosed the first world I was to know outside the United States.

Now it happened that the manuscript upon which I was working and from which I was diverted by Mrs. Slade's call dealt with the very subject of fieldwork. Tentatively entitled *Cognitive Dimensions of Fieldwork: The Metamorphosis of an Anthropologist*, the manuscript addressed my concern with the dwindling role of fieldwork in the current training of cultural anthropologists. Central to it was my conviction that fieldwork outside the United States is critical to the mind-set that distinguishes us as anthropologists from all other professionals and lays the foundation for our unique contribution to the knowledge of human behavior. Yet nowhere in the completed chapters of that manuscript was the reality of fieldwork, its personal and professional impact, as graphically conveyed as in my letters to my father.

I owe my reader the caution that in substance the letters were not at all profound. And lest I paint too darkly those anthropologists for whom distant fieldwork is viewed as increasingly "archaic" (the designation of one member of our department, distressed by my insistence on it), I alert the reader that my first fieldwork was not exemplary. I may well be the antianthropologist my children say I am: programmed for bad luck, genetically bereft of a sense of direction, plagued with a knack for being in the wrong country at the wrong time, and having an affinity for revolution, heat waves, and chaos. However, if anthropology converts to a vicarious dependence on data banks, and if fieldwork is "reprioritized" (in the vocabulary of my colleague) to optional ranking, I shall be saddened. And I shall be convinced that the profession is the poorer for it.

1

Fieldwork
A Rite of Passage

What follows is an account of my first fieldwork: a year of anthropological study in the fishing village of Taarnby (not the community's real name), Denmark. My purpose in writing is to convey something of the unpublished side of fieldwork, of that infrequently documented disparity between the experience of long-term fieldwork's months of effort and intimacy and the published accounts—often years later.

For graduate students in the late fifties there was no way, absolutely no way, of becoming a real anthropologist without foreign fieldwork, a hallowed rite of passage. Formal training in fieldwork was rare. Some degree of insight was provided by our professors in lectures, but the message conveyed was that the stuff of fieldwork was essentially incommunicable. Over the months and years of graduate work we were informed that you learned fieldwork by doing fieldwork. You learned by a process of immersion—marination is a better word—in jungles, swamps, and arctic floes. The fact that our professors were only sporadically articulate about their field ordeals contributed to the sense of mystery with which fieldwork was endowed.

Fieldwork was presented as a difficult, demanding business. In one year—as nearly as we could reconstruct it—our Peoples of Africa professor learned two unwritten languages, built his own hut, and maintained an uneasy peace between warlike tribes,

1

all the while gathering data on a village whose kinship structure was unparalleled in anthropological reporting.

Fieldwork loomed as an undertaking only a little less challenging than a self-performed appendectomy, a feat that one anthropologist—goaded, I suspect, beyond endurance by the one-upmanship of a colleague—said he had performed on himself in an Amazonian village. The fact that he performed it badly and was rushed by bearers through the jungle to a down-river hospital absolved him from self-glorification.

Sites for fieldwork ideally were desolate, snake-infested, malaria-ridden communities a hundred miles (minimally) from the nearest vestige of civilization. Our professors spoke with awesome familiarity about their villages, their mud-and-dung huts, their people, and their diseases.

Part of the mystique lay in the continuing implication that the skills critical to successful fieldwork anywhere in the world were essentially unimpartible. One could do fieldwork or one could not. "The field," as it was patronizingly referred to by those who had survived its challenges, separated the men from the boys, the sheep from the goats, the grain from the chaff. Like acne to the teenager, the dismay that pervaded a student's every pore on the eve of first fieldwork was viewed as an inevitable phase of this professional rite of passage. As graduate students we longed for the day when we would have our people, our huts, our villages, and our diseases: we wanted to be real anthropologists too.

As the period of my own dissertation fieldwork approached, my sense of personal competence stood in inverse relationship to the awe in which I held the men (I had no women professors) who had not only survived the field experience but had also lived to write acclaimed accounts of peoples whose language and culture they had mastered despite heavy odds. I yearned to join the ranks of these esoteric scholars and to experience the challenges critical to membership in their community. I asked the National Science Foundation to send me to Ghana—identified in a prominent encyclopedia of the period as "The White Man's Grave"—to study the changing status of the paramount chiefs in Ghana's Northern Territories.

The time was the late fifties. Research funding was then easier to obtain than it is now. Wars, if not fewer, were more respectably identified. And more often than not, as graduate students we were simply sent somewhere by our omniscient departments. I could scarcely endure the five months of waiting before I would learn whether or not my proposed Ghana research had been funded. I read voraciously on West Africa. The downside of possible funding was the prospect of separation from my husband, Thor, who had just received his doctorate in anthropology, and from my daughter Katie, then five years old.

Two months after I submitted my research proposal I learned I was again pregnant. I withdrew the Africa proposal from consideration, and at the end of the semester I left, with my anthropologist husband and my daughter, to do my first fieldwork in the village of Taarnby (pronounced "torn bee") on the diminutive Danish island of Amager in the Øresund, the turbulent sound which links the Baltic Sea and the Kattegat.

The research grant was Thor's, and it was a significant one anthropologically. For despite the resistance of purists and the legacy of tribal field sites, work in peasant villages of Latin America and Europe was achieving acceptance within anthropological departments, largely because of the exciting new theoretical directions emerging from the research. Some work within our own culture had also begun to nourish interdisciplinary theory in areas of culture change, ethnicity, and psychological anthropology. I was to assist Thor in documenting the cultural process that was transforming the tiny village's traditional dependence on the sea to a pattern of encroaching urbanization and dependence on nearby Copenhagen. The fieldwork became the basis for my own doctoral dissertation.

My mourning for Ghana and the brotherhood of tribal scholars was short-lived. I was happier to be in the field with Thor than separated from him (a common enough circumstance in the remarkably inbred world of anthropology, but one which contributes to a huge rate of marital instability and divorce among us). Katie thrived, and I thrived in my pregnancy.

The following chapters constitute neither a complete nor a dispassionate account of our year in Taarnby. Its fictionalized form makes the book aberrant as anthropology, so that from the outset I absolve myself of the responsibilities inherent in standard ethnographic reporting. Further, the reader seeking theoretical enlightenment is cautioned that the book is not meant to advance the anthropological literature derived from European studies. And although several joint scholarly publications did follow from our work in Denmark, this book is not one of them.

My motive throughout is to convey the seldom published side of fieldwork: to share with the reader on an intimate level some dimensions of the personal and professional sides of *first* fieldwork, which, despite some fine and relevant books, is inadequately documented. Some sensitive ethnographies make helpful reference to the difficulties and challenges inherent in first fieldwork, but for the most part by the time they are written, often five to ten years afterwards, the stories are told impersonally; the real legacy has been forgotten or subtly reprogrammed in the mind of the researcher. That this should be the case is defensible and not surprising. The day-to-day unvarnished script of fieldwork rarely lends itself to the level of abstraction appropriate to published accounts of it. In addition, a significant part of our training as anthropologists is committed to helping to make automatic the suppression of extraneous personal reporting.

However, first fieldwork, and much of later fieldwork as well, is not characterized by the orderly progression that is eventually bred into published accounts of it. The gap between the way it was in the field and the way it turns out to be in print is generally considerable. Graduate students would be helped very much, I think, by being candidly advised of this and reassured that even the most flagrant lapses from idealized standards of field procedure need not damn the research outcome.

Denmark presented less of a challenge than Ghana would have. No doubt about it. But for me Taarnby was a learning experience unmatched by anything that followed, anywhere in the world. Taarnby was first fieldwork.

Even for Thor, who at that time was one of only a handful of well-trained specialists in European research, the year was not without its murky periods. Thor arrived in Taarnby with previous experience in fieldwork and fluent in Danish, and if any prerequisite to fieldwork was to burn itself into my brain it was that of an adequate command of the field language before departure from one's university. I reached the field ill-prepared for work in Denmark, having had time to do little more than struggle through *You Can Say It in Danish*, a phrase book for tourists which armed me with such valuable phrases as "My glasses are broken" and "Give my regards to your aunt and uncle." In our initial weeks on the island I was to work these into local conversations with the greatest of difficulty.

2

⟡⟢

Getting Started
First Impressions

We had come to the village of Taarnby, Denmark, to do a study of culture change. The island's conservative inhabitants had destroyed a thriving maritime economy in the conviction that their sailing fleets, which fished the cold northern waters for herring and cod, would outlive the transient folly of steam- and gas-powered craft. Now, a half-century later, the isolated community maintained an otherworldliness. Its Hans Christian Andersen houses, packed into crooked and cobbled lanes, lent an air of enchantment that was intensified by the fog and mist which sifted into the harbor from the open sea and clung to the dark nets spread on beaches only slightly grayer than the sea around them. The harbor, once one of Denmark's busiest, sometimes sheltered as few as ten ships.

In the ritualized anthropological process known as participant observation, we lived for one year (on boiled eel and other delicacies from the sea) in a thatched two-story cottage (available because no fisherman would live in it) warmed by a single pot-bellied stove through a winter that froze the open sea and locked all sailing vessels in the long twilight of the subarctic.

Most fieldwork, I suspect, begins badly. More charitably I should perhaps state that my record in establishing field rapport is far from emulable. During our first month in Taarnby I was inadequate in everything I did. As a matter of fact, just plain inadequacy was a level of performance to which I aspired.

7

In the first week of residence, when in keeping with sound anthropological protocol we were bent on keeping a low profile, I routed Thor, Katie, and me out of our small thatched cottage into the street one morning in our nightclothes.

"What on earth happened?" Thor asked, as gray smoke emanated from every orifice of our little house. The three of us stood shifting our bare feet on the cobblestones. A moment before I had been tranquilly pushing rolled newspapers into our sluggish stove.

"Too much paper, I guess," I said. For with the first welcome flame I had forced my entire reserve of bow-knotted pages of newspaper into the potbellied *kakkelovn*. The belching soot floated across the fence and descended upon our neighbor's fresh morning washing as a parade of early schoolbound children ambled past, distracted from the spectacle by their parents, who discreetly avoided staring. It took two more ill-fated tries before our ancient stove gave up the secret of its predilection for a load of half-wood and half-coke—a costly combination in an area virtually denuded of trees.

The following afternoon, having spent the day mapping the location of houses, stores, fishermen's shacks, and other structures (a preliminary phase of fieldwork), I decided to treat myself to a cup of coffee in the dining room of the community's only hotel. Pride of the village, the hotel had been remodeled recently, and new broad glass windows allowed an unobstructed view of the harbor and beyond it the red-striped sails of the pilot boats that guided ocean-going craft bound for the ports of Copenhagen or Elsinore through the treacherously narrow channel of the sound.

"Coffee," I said, and the waiter raced off, apparently as reluctant to test my Danish further as I was to attempt it.

Enthusiastic with my morning's productivity, I spread the map across the tabletop, imagining it completed and occupying a prominent place in a lovely, scholarly treatise that would electrify the anthropological world. Suddenly I was intrigued by a brown circle centrally located on the paper. I wondered what it was doing there and why it was growing ever larger even as I looked at it. Too late came the realization of what the pungent odor and crackling sound had already conveyed to a startled dining room and to my quick-witted waiter, who raced across the room, pitcher of water in hand. I had, in my reverie, lowered the map onto one of the votive-candle lamps that provided a decorous tone to the new "continental" dining room decor. As flames leaped from the map I could see the erect figures of restaurant guests looming about its edges, arms in the air, like stylized bodies in a cave painting. I clung hypnotically, riveted to the disappearing map. Then I felt a sharp slap to my wrist as a man forced from my hands the burning fragments. They fell to the white tablecloth, just as my rescuer and I felt the full impact of the waiter's pitcher of ice water upon us. The man was the chief pilot of the village, and by morning, news of the event had spread through the village as the little thatched community girded itself for winter with a pyromaniac.

The experience was devastating. Years and several field experiences would pass before the comforting recognition would come that the dreadful volatility of first days in the field is rooted in the dynamics of culture contact and only tangentially effected by levels of professional adequacy. It is impossible to separate the observer from the observed in the initiation of contact into one another's worlds. In Taarnby, the more mundane the dimension of daily life in which we found ourselves tested, the more wonderingly we were regarded by the villagers. My behavior invited particular awe. I found myself frustrated in the most casual attempts at participant observation (for which I was appropriately primed). Observe what? The only thing the villagers seemed to be doing was observing me—cautiously.

Fortunately, Thor was effecting a soothing counterinfluence. A tall, ruggedly handsome man, he struck that balance between forcefulness and placidity that Danes adore. What I lacked in predictability he abundantly projected. After breakfast each day he would take off across the village on his scheduled rounds: the marketplace, the harbor, the "green" where the fishermen dried and mended their nets and where a great and menacing gaggle of geese were kept for their eggs and fattened for the coming winter feasts. Afternoons he had appointments with many of the old-timers through whose memories, diaries, and letters we were reconstructing the past.

He returned during the third week of our residence with precious information on the local school system, and I managed to get Katie enrolled in kindergarten. She was enthusiastic about the prospect. I was distraught, weighing all the advantages of getting her placed against the psychological mayhem that might follow her plunge into a different language universe. Thor said comforting things when I returned to the cottage without her, but he wasn't smiling either.

I began frequenting the most innocuous places I could find for study, like the church and the cemetery, trying to rebuild my image. The time spent was rewarding. Cemeteries, I learned, provide useful insights on family structure within a community, on family wealth, and on generational links with the past. The Lutheran pastor welcomed the interest he read into my visits. Over the months of our stay his verbal documentary on the church's history clarified the demography of immigration, marriage, politics, and war that had culminated in Taarnby's present population. Success in fieldwork, I began to appreciate, is advanced by respect for its sometimes serendipitous nature. Little by little the fieldworker eventually cultivates an aptitude for making fortunate discoveries.

I was acquiring a Spartan vocabulary and a limited but workable command of verbs. However, the Danish spoken on our island derived from a dialect once common in the entire sound, with a tonality added by early immigrants from north Holland. Its singsongy cadence was enough to render me nearly mute for the first two months of our sojourn. My occasional attempts to engage in casual conversation were aborted by seizures of shyness.

I had been assured before leaving the United States that everyone in Denmark spoke English—another myth to be laid to rest alongside the legend that Danish pastry originated and achieved mastery in that country. The "Viennese breads," as they were called in Denmark and as they were baked by local housewives, would have made adequate doorstops.

Only three people on the island spoke English. The physician's knowledge was pure "dictionary translation." Thus placing a stethoscope on Katie's chest, he told her to "respire profoundly, please!"—a directive to which she immediately and ably responded. The butcher's knowledge was limited to some English words for Danish meats and their preparation. However, the meat was butchered into cuts which apparently did not translate, and in their uncooked state, they bore no resemblance to anything

I had ever seen laid out on a Safeway counter. Beef was apparently unknown. Most of the limited, visible inventory of meats shone with the delicate patina of old silver. Nor were words for broil, bake, or roast worth the struggle when all that my kitchen contained was a two-plate burner. Eventually Knud, the butcher, took to fleeing into the refrigerator when I entered the shop, until—aided by his partner—I mercifully pointed to something, had it wrapped, and left to ponder what to do with it in the privacy of our cottage.

The third person who spoke English must surely have been eligible for canonization by the time of our departure. Tove had lived for fifteen years in Saskatchewan, married to a Canadian farmer. Sometimes when my brain ached and my eyes fogged over with the unrelieved discipline of forcing my childlike Danish to the needs of fieldwork, I would run to her house and sit and let the sound of her English wash over me. Tove was garrulous. I needed only to nod my head. And I would stay in her minuscule parlor on a sofa plumped with hand-sewn pillows, half-listening to recipes and gossip, until at last refreshed and recharged, I could go out into the streets again and face the complex civilities of Danish greetings and proper Danish life.

After nearly two months of snaillike progress, I decided to find some low-keyed activity that would involve me casually, but more acceptably and challengingly, in village life. Something that would allow me to exercise my Danish beyond the formal questionnaire interviews I had begun with the wives of pilots, fishermen, and maritime crews.

Thor and I conferred. He suggested that I should enroll in the cooking class offered for adults at the local high school on Monday and Thursday evenings from six to nine o'clock. It seemed a brilliant idea. I would learn what to do with all that strangely dissected meat and with those fish—great and small— that lay languidly shimmering, eyes staring, on enormous wood trays in the harbor. I would make the sweet soups Thor was so fond of: buttermilk, apricot, and beer soup with whipped cream and ground black bread. And I would ask why they had rid the island of vegetables and fruits.

Above all, I wanted to create a tray of those exquisite smørrebrød sandwiches, as complex as a medieval still life, perfectly crafted in line and color. And our home would become a mecca for the pastry-obsessed housewives of the village, who could chat for hours about the appropriate icing for a cupcake.

The time was right. A new class was to begin the following week.

3

Participant Observation

Cooking School

I have fictionalized the characters and places that were so much a part of daily life in Taarnby. Local homes and scenes, like friends and neighbors, have been jigsawed into a reality protective of actual identity. Where there is risk of embarrassment, real events are dramatized within created contexts that obscure them from easy recognition. The most important criterion for inclusion was whether the telling of it helps the reader better to comprehend the frustrations and the satisfactions of first fieldwork.

Published ethnographic accounts of fieldwork seem so sure. As a graduate student I marveled at the confident progression of logic that distinguished the many ethnographies we were assigned, from the first scrupulously descriptive chapters to the final theoretical explication of the research findings. Page followed page in a mounting avalanche of supportive evidence to the monograph's culminating and erudite listing of references cited. Behind such accounts, undeniably, lay lucid, first-rate minds. My fieldwork was never to reflect that clarity of insight, and my expectation that it should was for many years the most inhibiting part of my field experience. In the context of first fieldwork, life in Taarnby was life in a mine field from the beginning. My most careful efforts seemed routinely to achieve a quality somewhere between Liza Crossing the Ice and A Night at the Opera.

On the following Monday, I dressed for Taarnby School's adult cooking class. I changed my clothes three times before deciding on a camel-colored sweater and skirt. Over them I wore my venerable dyed-lamb coat, for Thor had warned me, "That place will be like an icebox."
Set among the thatched, peaked-roof cottages, the school building with its poured-concrete architecture looked as alien as a spaceship. I couldn't have been more nervous if I had been going to a ball at Fredensborg Castle. Clutching a small, folded apron, I found it was no easy matter to locate the front door, let alone the classroom. There seemed no break at all in the flat facade. I moved back into the middle of the cobbled street to try to get some perspective just in time for a man to maneuver his bicycle around me and dismount.
"Hello," he said, whisking his bicycle onto a rack.
"I don't suppose you'd know where the cooking school meets," I said.
"The door is just to the side," he gestured. "I am going there, too." He moved rapidly ahead of me and then turned as I stood weighing his pronouncement. "Come! Come!" he urged. "The teacher is called 'Talia the Terrible.' She will have our heads if we are late."
I followed him through a tunnellike entrance to the far side of the building that took us through double doors down a short corridor and into the classroom, bright with light and with white tiles that covered the floor and walls to a height of about eight feet. It looked rather like an empty swimming pool, except that almost at the point of entrance and running crosswise stood a great table with chairs around it. And behind it a half-dozen smaller tables for four were spaced to form a kind of restaurant. Along the far wall were several stoves. Sinks banked both sides of the room. On each side of the sinks were work surfaces, and above them cupboards had somehow been affixed to the tiles.
I shall never forget our teacher, Fru Rasmussen, alias Talia the Terrible. When she turned her full gaze upon me I forgot every word of Danish I knew. Except that she was half-again as tall and three times as wide, she reminded me of Helen Hayes as she

looked in the late-show reruns of A Farewell to Arms, standing competently in the hospital ward in the uniform and headdress of a World War I nurse.

Fru Rasmussen was laminated into an unsulliable white buttoned-front dress that extended almost to her ankles and was of such stiffness that the elbow-length sleeves encircled, but did not touch, the skin of her generous arms. A triangle of the same taut cotton hid all but an inch of her iron-gray hair. Impassively, she lifted a large black cigar to her lips and waited for us to find seats.

"Abject apologies," said my guide, and I mumbled a repetition of his words. We slipped into the only two vacant chairs that remained, so positioned that they afforded a profile view of Fru Rasmussen, who from that angle looked as if—perhaps without the cigar—she might be affixed to the prow of a sailing ship. Except for my cyclist friend, the class was female, and there were perhaps a dozen of us.

"Exactly twelve!" said Fru Rasmussen, who I was now convinced could read my thoughts. "And that is good," she continued. "Three tables of four. At every class we shall prepare a complete meal of four courses, with each person at a table responsible for one course. In this fashion each table prepares and consumes a full dinner. You will, therefore, not eat before you come. You will not smoke during the preparation, cooking, or consumption of food. Tobacco is permitted before or after class or during our ten-minute break."

We were then advised to choose our foursomes. With more tables than arithmetically feasible, given the four to-a-table directive, we had a problem from the start. What ensued was an aberrant version of musical chairs as women anxiously circled the tables, weighing the consequences of where and with whom they might suddenly find themselves irrevocably seated. The first sorting produced two persons at five tables, with the bicycle rider and I left standing. Fru Rasmussen's left arm slashed the air with the precision of a symphony conductor.

"Be seated," she ordered. If she had in the same tone ordered me to leap to a tabletop, I should unhesitatingly have done so.

The bicycle rider and I quickly sat at an occupied table directly in front of us, thereby producing the first foursome—like some significant mutation in a precipitous evolutionary change. There followed a disorganized shuffling about as nervous partners rapidly occupied vacant chairs lest they be separated. At one point six women converged on an empty table that went to the swiftest and fittest. Eventually the remaining women faltered into place.

Her next directive was to "put on the smocks!" I knew this word only because a smock was a portion of the uniform required of schoolchildren.

My apron evoked a wan smile from Fru Rasmussen. "Charming," she said. And then, "On Thursday, a smock!"

We were shown where utensils, bowls, cutlery, and china were kept. We paid our fees and our names were entered into a ledger according to table membership, an undertaking that constituted a mass, informal introduction. Socially we were roughing it. And I thanked God. True and proper Danish introductions require a complex etiquette which legitimizes the compulsive need of Danes to know everything about one another.

My cycling friend was Poul, an engineer. He was from the beginning entirely comfortable in a class of women. When Grete, whom I recognized as the assistant postmistress, ventured that he must be a gourmet, Poul said matter-of-factly, "Oh no! Not at all. It's simply that my wife is a dreadful cook."

Grete shook her head sympathetically.

"Oh, it's quite understandable," Poul continued. "You see she *hates* to cook. Always has, really."

He was buttoning himself into what looked like a white lab coat. It apparently passed inspection by Talia the Terrible, who accorded Poul one of her rare smiles.

So we were four. In addition to Grete, Poul, and I, there was Inge, who was blond and pretty and planning to be married as soon as she and her fiancé could find a place to live in Copenhagen, where he worked as apprentice to a silversmith. Inge was as assertive as Grete was timid. Poul was simply forthright. It seemed to me a fortuitous group, congenial and united. Together we should not be a total pushover for Talia the Terrible's juggernaut approach to Danish high cuisine.

We began with what I thought a humble enough assignment. Cucumber salad, meat loaf, potatoes, and a sweetened berry compote which is to Denmark what Jello is to the United States. Fortunately, or unfortunately as it turned out, the meat loaf was assigned to me—a decision that left the rest of the table faintly awed.

Food terms are a hellish but critical challenge in any language. If you can develop the faintest comfort with a culture's food vocabulary, with the words used for everyday fare, festive fare, spices, beverages, food for children, food for the sick, hot weather food, cold weather food, the never-to-eat foods (which in Denmark give you anything from hives to night blindness), you are halfway to bilingualism if you never learn another word. My Danish Made Simple listed thirty varieties of fish alone, only two of which I could identify with confidence, the eel and the stingray, and then only in their raw states. Why twenty-five vegetables and twenty fruits were listed I could not imagine, though I dutifully tried to commit them to memory. In two months I had seen or tasted only red cabbage, carrots, cucumbers, the ubiquitous potato (often prepared in two or three ways for a single meal), and lumpy apples, which got that way from being stored after harvest for months on attic floors and rotated lest they rot.

However, that first evening at cooking class I felt welling up within me an alien and buoyant sense of confidence. "I think this is going to be great," I told Poul.

Fru Rasmussen's kitchen was very orderly. Virtually everything was labeled. All the canisters. All the utensils. Even the great wire whisk had a sliver of paper affixed to its handle to assure that its identity was in no way to be a source of perplexity to the uninitiated. Henceforth it and other terms would be engraved on my mind, and in this easy fashion my vocabulary would soar in no time at all.

Each table was assigned its own inviolable work surface, ample and deep enough for four to work beside the stoves.

"In the preparation of dinner, it shall be my practice," said Fru Rasmussen, "to read aloud to the assembled class instructions for all courses." We were admonished to listen always "with all ears." After her oral instructions, she would hand a detailed recipe, typed on a card, to the appropriate chef.

"Each of you will be assigned a chef-and-table title. Thus, tonight Fru Anderson will be Meat Loaf Chef Two. 'Meat Loaf,' since at her table the responsibility for the main dish will fall on her. And 'Two,' since she occupies the table bearing the marker two." She nodded in my direction, reaffirming the assignment she had seen fit to allot me. Perhaps I was not on her hit list after all.

"Students will be addressed and will address one another by their chef-and-table titles," she continued in staccato tones. Use of Christian names or surnames (like the use of tobacco) was henceforth restricted to off-duty breaks.

Ingredients needed in the preparation of dinner were housed in open shelves above us; utensils were in open shelves below. There were curious miniature clipboards at fixed locations on the wall above each chef's work space, and to these appropriate recipes were to be attached. The location was high but readable for me. It was definitely at crouch level for Poul. In those first intense moments at our recipes, peering from odd positions, we must all have looked like a pack of hapless voyeurs.

There were two more ironclad rules: first, regardless of the oral presentation—made by Fru Rasmussen—one's own recipe was to be read from start to finish before one did anything in the kitchen; second, ingredients were to be gathered and used in the order of their listing unless instructions were given to the contrary.

The entire class was in action before I had finished the required reading of the recipe. It seemed a strange combination for meat loaf, but I knew the Danish predilection for sweets. If not swift, I was sure. I even drew a smile from Fru Rasmussen as she watched me scrape a knife across the top of a measuring cup. Thinking in grams and kilos normally gave me enormous difficulty, but tonight I was having no problems.

"You will all take a moment to observe Meat Loaf Chef Two," Fru Rasmussen commanded, "as she carefully but gently assures no more nor less than the required amount."

I felt very good and turned to beating two eggs (next item) authoritatively into the bowl. There followed an impressive sequence of spices whose names I could not translate and only two of which I could identify with certainty, salt and pepper.

Since the meat loaf would be the longest cooking, and since its chefs had been enjoined "to get on with it," I began to feel some pressure to keep pace with my colleagues, particularly when I heard oven doors opening and closing around me. I beat the ground veal and pork together with unrelenting strokes, though my arm was growing tired and heavy. Finally, having slid the pan into the small black and white oven, I joined the others and listened to the small talk about our coming feast.

Fru Rasmussen lit up another large black cigar. One woman smoked a smaller brown version that was in common use in the village. Poul lit his pipe. There was a pitcher of water and a tray of glasses. We all drank copiously.

The room had begun to heat up as the ovens reached their "moderately hot" temperatures. The wool skirt and sweater had been a mistake. I walked over and leaned against the tiles. Poul opened the back door and there was a rush of cool air, smelling of the sea. The women walked about, studying the cupboards and their contents.

Suddenly Fru Rasmussen lifted her left wrist, displaying her watch, and tapped the face of it with a fingernail. It had the clear finality of the timed seizure of the guns of Navarone. "Meat Loaf Chefs will check their . . ." and there followed a word I could not understand. "The others will proceed to the setting of tables."

While Fru Rasmussen expounded on table settings and the intricacies of napkin folding (a Danish compulsion), I cautiously followed the Meat Loaf Chefs so that I might determine, undetected, the precise mission that had been assigned us. They touched nothing on or in the stove, but peered at what I immediately but belatedly recognized as timers fixed on the back panels. And at that precise moment I heard their joint ticking like the relentless activity of some agitated bomb.

I had not set my timer! I didn't even remember reading about a timer. Not that I would have recognized the word, but it must have been there somewhere, or maybe I had missed it in Fru Rasmussen's rapid verbal instructions. "How many minutes?" came Fru Rasmussen's voice.

"Twenty-seven! Twenty-five! Twenty-eight!" came the replies of the other Meat Loaf Chefs. There were a few heavy seconds of silence. And then I leaned with simulated interest over my stove, studying the back panel. "Thirty!" I called aloud. As it was, I had probably shaved four minutes off my actual baking time. Fru Rasmussen cocked her head to one side, giving full consideration to standard meat loaf deviations. For a moment I thought she was going to leave the group that was pulling dishes and flatwear from the cupboards.

My heart was hammering. If she approached my stove, I intended to either slump to the floor, feigning heat prostration—a condition I was rapidly approaching anyway—or chance it and whirl the timer knob to thirty minutes. What disturbed me was that I had no idea how prominent a noise the latter course of action would create, but somehow it seemed a more dramatic move than the first.

Fortunately for everyone, she remained where she was and announced: "Napkin time! All chefs to the main table!"

For the next fifteen minutes we were occupied with making graceful white swans from starched white napkins—a feat I executed once but was never to duplicate. When at last the tables were properly set and inspected, the Salad Chefs had their moment. To them would routinely fall the additional responsibilities of "presenting" bread and butter and whatever condiments were appropriate to the meal. There were courteous *ohs* and *ahs* over the marinated cucumbers which had been scraped and sliced into delicate snowflake patterns.

Dinner was announced and we sat down. Fru Rasmussen sat at a separate table, the better to review and display samples from the efforts of each chef. A segmented dish, of the kind used at picnics, that keeps beans from running into salad, lay before her, except that hers was large indeed and had numerous sections. The four Salad Chefs had already deposited samples of their cucumbers for her review. Our individual servings lay in their cool delicacy in small dishes before each of us. Fru Rasmussen speared a single cucumber and I could resist no longer. The cucumbers were lovely, if few, and I devoured them in several strokes of the fork.

"Before beginning our salads," Fru Rasmussen started. I looked around our table. With their eyes mercifully lowered Poul and Grete and Inge were waiting. As was everyone else. I replaced my fork on my dish and the small sound reverberated from the tiles. "Before beginning our salads," Fru Rasmussen began again.

Poul looked distracted. "I smell something," he said quite audibly. Inge nodded. "Meat loaf."

"No," Poul said. Grete nodded her agreement. "It smells more like . . . carmelized potatoes."

"Before beginning our salads," Fru Rasmussen said again,

enunciating now with clear displeasure. Her eyes were riveted on Poul.

"I know that smell," Poul persisted. "Browning sugar."

People were beginning to say that they smelled something. And then, before I could figure out why I found these pronouncements troubling, there was a great ping!

"Meat Loaf Chefs to the ovens," Fru Rasmussen called out, and I was on my feet, adrenalin coursing. Something in the back of my mind was surfacing, something with which my brain was struggling but was oddly reluctant to confront.

The stoves with their spindly iron legs and black and white enameled ovens suddenly looked as Danish and foreign as the schoolhouse flag. Apprehension lay on me like a damp towel. We were handed potholders. We opened the oven doors and, as directed, carried the pans wreathed in steam to our tables, where we placed them on tiles provided especially for them.

I walked, my pan wreathed not only in steam but in a powerfully emanating sweetness that soon penetrated the room like cheap perfume.

"It's rather dark for meat loaf, isn't it?" said Grete. It shone, glistening like a small iridescent oil spill.

"However did you do that?" Poul asked, impressed. By now my meat loaf had attracted an audience. I went over to check the meat loaves at other tables. They were brown and much more plumped up. They did not shine. There was considerable milling about until Fru Rasmussen called for order. One had the feeling she was less in command of things.

The white segmented sampling plate began circulating through the tables, picking up meat loaf samples as it went. Ours was the last.

"I'll do it," said Inge in the low, supportive voice one uses in the presence of the bereaved. She poised a dinner knife over the end of the meat loaf. The first gentle sawing produced nothing. She raised the knife, tip sharply downward, penetrating the meat at a right angle. The second thrust produced the kind of shattering one sees in vandalized unbreakable glass; the third, a portion of meat from which hung a kind of peanut brittle jacket. Inge placed it on the plate and the jacket fell back into place. I took the plate from her hands and carried it to Fru Rasmussen. A palpable silence had fallen over the room.

We agreed later that Fru Rasmussen displayed uncharacteristic gentleness. I believe she was in shock, but she was diplomatic when she spoke to me. "I am curious as to what innovations you brought to the recipe," she said—as nearly as I could translate.

If my Danish had been up to it, I would have told her that it was all I could do to keep up with the barrage of instructions, let alone embark on creative embroidery of them. Under the circumstances, my vocabulary shrank like some shaken thermometer to a new low, as it did under all situations of pressure. I did the only thing I could think of. I took Fru Rasmussen by the arm and steered her to the stove, above which still hung the fateful recipe. I stared at it as one might stare at the formula for a strychnine-laced cocktail. Within it, somehow, lay a dreadful secret.

With a precision born of muteness I pointed to the first ingredient and released my grip on her arm long enough to describe with thumbs and index fingers the arcs of two eggs. Then, resuming my grasp, I resolutely directed her eyes to the second listing, at which point I used both hands to lower the large canister of sugar. I placed it on the work counter and scrounged about until I found the four-gram measuring cup. I generated a forced smile to reenact her public praise of the precision with which I had expertly scraped my knife across the dry measure of sugar.

Then I hit an impasse. Meat. How to convey the proportions of veal and pork? Poul was at my side, and I found my voice "What is it?" I asked.

There followed a very rapid exchange between Poul and Fru Rasmussen. Then Fru Rasmussen turned her full gaze upon me. But it was Poul who spoke:

"Say 'sugar.'"

"Mel," I said.

"Say 'flour.'"

"Melis."

"Close," Poul said. Then he turned, translating the exchange for Fru Rasmussen. A low moan escaped her lips as we both realized how, by confounding "sugar" with "flour," I had desecrated the meat loaf.

Eventually the class did get around to laughing, although not heartily. Since dinner at school had to serve as a real meal twice a week for the next six weeks, I loomed as a clear and constant menace. I had broken a cardinal rule of Danish culture: never stand between a Dane and his dinner. Further, as Thor would point out: a hungry Dane is one who has only eaten enough for one. On that first evening, the generous dessert, expertly prepared by Poul, tempered but did not alleviate concern about my presence.

At the next class I was made a Dessert Chef, a legitimate rotation except that I was charged with watching all the puddings cool on the chilly back stairs, ostensibly to insure their safety from animal predators. Actually it was a serious demotion. Another Dessert Chef assumed the cooking responsibility for our table.

At the third meeting I was restored to service as Soup Chef Two. Chowder was on the menu, and like each of the Soup Chefs, I had the initial assignment of preparing the soup stock. Members of my table and other Soup Chefs gave me warm pats on the back and said encouraging things which only reinforced my feeling of being on probation. "We are with you all the way," Inge whispered as I slipped into my smock.

The first step in preparing the chowder was surgically removing the eyes from four large fish heads. Fru Rasmussen stood at my side ready to direct my hands through this routine procedure. She outlined with her finger the appropriate incision in the tissue of the head.

"He is very fresh," she said. "See how bright and clear the eye! If you do it properly, the eyes will simply pop into your hands."

The eye was bright and clear and fixed on me. I looked around the room at all the busy Soup Chefs. "Proceed," Fru Rasmussen said, taking firm hold of my fish. I picked up the knife and lowered the point of the blade to the fish head.

"Well?" said Fru Rasmussen.

I looked up and saw a woman open a bloody hand and drop something into a bucket. I heard "Pong! Ping!" as the objects hit bottom.

Then—as nearly as I remember—I took off my smock, solemnly shook hands with each of my tablemates (as good form requires), said goodbye to Fru Rasmussen, put on my lambskin coat, and walked out into the icy Danish night.

Poul and Grete and Inge forgave me and carried on as a threesome. At Christmas Poul invited our family to join his in a traditional goose dinner with all the trimmings—a meal he fixed himself.

My reputation as a high school cooking class dropout generated surprisingly favorable dividends. There was a consensus. No one as incompetent as I was could continue to be regarded as a serious threat to village life. The chief pilot's wife, who had eluded my attempts to arrange an interview with her, came to call and in the course of her visit volunteered to teach me some of her family's favorite recipes. She was happy to do it, she insisted, "for the sake of the family."

I concluded that the village wives had drawn straws to stave off the starvation of my unfortunate husband and child, and that the chief pilot's wife, Fru Strunge, had gotten the short straw.

Things were looking up.

4

Demands of Daily Living
The Bathhouse

As an anthropologist, I do lay claim to an inventory of modest virtues that have served me well in the field over the years. These were perhaps best summarized by a student who—in a routine written evaluation of one of my courses—observed that I was amiable, informed, persevering, and clean.

Cleanliness is a virtue whose sustained pursuit in the field is rarely documented in published reports. Even in Scandinavia, a culture enamored of the bath—wholesome and invigorating refinements of which have been widely adopted in America's finest homes—there remain vast inhabitated areas where the daily bath is unknown.

On the island of Taarnby, keeping clean, by standards with which I was familiar and which I struggled to perpetuate, was troublesome. For as the weeks progressed, keeping Katie, our clothes, and myself clean was consuming frightening amounts of time—time I would have preferred to spend in the pursuit of ethnographic enlightment. Katie, who was now well entrenched and thriving in kindergarten, had created for me the unanticipated opportunity for informal interviews with her teacher in exchange for an occasional "tale from America" during the class's daily story hour. I had become friendly with parents of several of the children, as well, paving the way for sessions with

25

them. With only a twelve-inch-square sink in the unheated kitchen and a single cold-water tap, bathing for Thor and me was limited to sponge baths. We did acquire a metal tub large enough to accommodate Katie in a knees-bent position. A wraparound head section had been designed to protect the young bather from drafts, and we would position the tub in the living room as close as possible to the potbellied *kakkelovn*. But since we only had two gas burners, most of an hour was needed to heat enough water to half fill it. Emptying the tub meant dragging it through the living room to the garden or bailing into the sink until the tub was manageable enough to lift.

I seemed to be forever boiling water toward the elusive goal of well-scrubbed bodies and clothes. I observed our neighbors and their children with frank appreciation of their ability to maintain both dimensions of cleanliness without heroic display. Of course, as Thor pointed out, most families were using the public showers in the schoolhouse—an experience I had resisted.

"It is time to simplify our lives," Thor announced with finality one day. When my eyes opened wide in the beginning of a protest, he led me from the water-soaked kitchen floor into the living room. He sat me down and held my hands.

"I know you're shy about this, but think of warm water, copious, unlimited amounts of warm water pouring over your *whole body.*" He put his arms around me. "You can do it. I know you can. Besides, as an anthropologist, can you really leave Denmark without experiencing a bath Danish style?"

"Oh Thor," I said. "It's not that I'm all that shy, it's just that— well, it's just that it's all so public here. I mean these are villagers that we work with day after day. It's not like going into a bathhouse full of *strangers.*"

Thor bounded away from me. "Hey! Why didn't I think of that. Terrific! We'll go into Copenhagen. Of course! Honey, you're really going to experience a bath, Danish style. An initiation into the ritual of the bath in the best possible context."

"Copenhagen?"

"You can't leave Denmark without having the works at the Copenhagen Baths. It's an institution. As old as the monarchy. Pure luxury, I promise you. Why, one afternoon, and you'll be addicted. And you'll take the Taarnby showers in your stride."

He lifted me from the floor in a bear hug. "I promise you an afternoon you'll never forget!"

There was in Thor a childlike delight in spontaneous gestures of love. I could see that he truly wanted this more for me than for his own pleasure. It was a sweetness that melted all resistance. "Oh God!" I said.

And so, on an ugly afternoon when the heavy rain made fieldwork unappealing, we arranged to drop Katie off with the Jensens, whose daughter was also in Fru Arentoft's kindergarten class (and whose family diaries dating from the 1890s Thor was in the process of reading). Thor and I headed for the city.

The bathhouse occupied almost a half-block on the edge of downtown Copenhagen. The front of it was like a theater with a small sign listing a range of prices, one of which, Thor told me, included a nap in a fine bed and bedside service of a bottle of well-chilled Danish beer. There was a box office in which a woman sat flanked by suspended rolls of brightly colored tickets. These she dispensed to an intermittent stream of people who were clearly regulars and knew unhesitatingly what they wanted.

"Can you get us two large hot tubs?" I asked.

"No bed?"

"No bed," I laughed. "No beer."

I watched him walk halfway to the window and then come back. He'd been thinking. "Listen, don't you want the works?" he said. "Not bed or beer, but the deluxe ticket which gives you a shower, a steam bath, and then your hot tub. Moneywise we're talking pennies."

There was excitement in his voice. He seemed so eager that I should enjoy myself in this marvelous experience that was familiar to him and unfamiliar to me. The rain was horizontal. All I could think of was warmth, being enveloped unqualifiedly and effortlessly in warmth and water.

"Sure," I said. "Why not? The works!"

He said, "Oh boy!" and was off. He returned with one red and one blue ticket. He gave me the red one. "This will get you in the women's side, over there," he gestured. "I have to take this door to the men's side, and we'll meet here at, say," he looked at his watch, "four o'clock. We'll have time for a cup of coffee before we head back."

"The women's side?" My mind had gotten no further than those words. "Sure," Thor said. "If you get the deluxe, that's the way you do it. A regular bath just has a private room with a couple of tubs. Four o'clock," he repeated. He gave me a kiss and took off in happy anticipation.

I walked through the double doors of the women's entrance, a little less convivial and only vaguely troubled as to the eventual disposition of a little packet of powdered soap I had been handed, together with a small pink bar and a plastic shower cap. I stopped before a booth. It looked like a checkroom so I slipped off my coat and lay it on the counter. A woman appeared, took my red ticket, and wordlessly handed me a steel bracelet with the number 11 on a silver disc dangling from the center of it. She also returned my coat and waved a casual hand to the right.

I took this as a cue and moved along the marble corridor. There were no numbers but at last an aisle and a series of polished wood doors. The first was marked with a blue-enameled 1, and in the second aisle, well back, I found 11. The door opened to a cubbyhole about 2 feet by 3 feet. There was a single clothes hook and a small mirror, and from the back of the door a folding bench dropped into place.

Where I wondered, did one get the towel and clogs to wear into the steam room? I went out into the corridor just as a woman in a pale blue dress approached the booth. She looked official. I waved my silver bracelet at her, pointing significantly to the 11, intending to convey my plight as soon as I could come up with a translation for "clogs." She stared at me, then with a hesitant smile, waved a silver bracelet of her own and disappeared from view down another aisle. I went back to 11 and removed my dress.

Five minutes elapsed. I could hear distant voices and the sound of water. Leaving my coat and dress in the room, I stepped once more into the hall, soap and shower cap in my hands. I turned off the main corridor to face a clerk with the name of the bathhouse embroidered in red and blue on a breast pocket.

"No! No!" she said in rapid Danish, clearly pained by my appearance. "Not with clothes!" And she marched me back to 11. "Not with clothes," she said again, smiling but insistent. She tugged at my slip, indicating I should remove it. Then she turned to go, but I held her in a steely grip.

It was my intention to explain that, were I to comply with her request, I should need some form of cover, and none had been provided me. I spoke rapidly, and I'm sure imperfectly, attempting graphic gestures of my plight with my free hand. Her brows furrowed, but then in a no-nonsense voice she repeated once more, "Not with clothes."

I stepped into the booth, removed my bra, panties, and hose, and took one last look in the mirror. Then, with the bar and packet of soap in one hand and the shower cap and bracelet in the other, I stepped into the hall.

I passed the attendant at her post. She smiled in broad approval, took the silver bracelet with 11 from my hand, placed it around my wrist, and motioned that I should follow. A turn to the right, a turn to the left, and we faced a pair of frosted doors. As she pushed them open into a room active with the splashing of some twenty nude women, I heard her loud and clear Danish in the only words I was fully to comprehend for the rest of the afternoon, "Here comes an American lady." And twenty heads lifted as one as I stepped into the white-tiled public bath, and the frosted doors closed behind me.

"Good afternoon," I waved, and headed for the open showers.

Another attendant materialized to head me off. "No, no!" she said. "You may not!" She checked my bracelet and led me to a bank of wooden pigeonholes, much like those one sees behind a hotel desk. There she took my bracelet and my soap from me, tucking the bracelet into hole number 11. I followed her and my soap to a great marble trough. Along the length of the trough were little tin basins. Into one of these she dumped the packet of powdered soap, filled the basin, handed it to me, and disappeared.

I observed the women observing me. They were scrubbing away with great brown wads. I moved quite close to the nearest lady, basin in hand, to study the wad, wrinkling my forehead to express desolate perplexity. "What is that?" I asked. She motioned across the room. "That there," she gestured.

The room was a steamy gray-white blur. I began a slow, scrutinizing approach. More basins, showers (which had been forbidden me), and then a great bin filled with a curly brown mass. Wood peelings, a kind of excelsior. A nude woman appeared. She dipped her hand into the bin, pulled loose a fistful of excelsior, and went back to the trough of tin basins. I followed her. From a recess under the trough she removed a small stool about a foot high which she carried to an alcove with a floor drain. There, hand basin beside her, she began an orderly scrubbing of her arms and legs, shaping with her hands small wads of excelsior which she rubbed vigorously on her skin. There followed intermittent little splashes from the basin as one area apparently passed inspection and she was ready to move on to the next with a newly compacted wad of wood cuttings.

My wrist was beginning to ache from holding the basin of soapy water in a level position. I pulled out a little stool of my own and with new confidence found an alcove, placed the stool in it authoritatively, and placed the basin on top of the stool. Then I headed back to the bin with its apparent load of wood by-products. A convenient loop extended like a long Shirley Temple curl. I pulled at it, felt some resistance, and pulled in earnest. A yard-long wad heaved itself over the edge of the bin and fell to the floor like the nest of some giant pterodactyl. The lady in uniform appeared as though shot through the floor, and there was another "you may not!" I headed back to my basin, excelsiorless.

There I was, still unwashed and with failing prospects that I ever would be. I looked dejectedly at the showers which had no handles of any kind that I could see. But my period of quiet contemplation was short-lived. I felt a slashing along a swath of skin from the base of my neck to the tip of my spine, and I turned to find the attendant, smiling amiably, a wad of excelsior in her hand, still completing the downward sweep which now scraped a layer of skin from my navel to my knee. "No! No! You may not!" I yelled. But she was swift and sure. By the time I realized what she intended it was too late. Worse, in my panic I ducked. The basin of water, intended for my torso, struck me full in the face, sloshing soap down over skin that glowed like a Cortes sunset.

I limped to the shower. By now I had attracted a small entourage to whom it had become obvious I would not survive without more orderly supervision. The handleless showers, they demonstrated, operated with a foot peddle that released a timed dose of water of regulated temperature. The scrubbed areas of my body turned to wide bands of crimson. I stepped out from under the shower and padded cautiously to the far end of the room. Somewhere along the way I had lost my shower cap, and my dripping hair further distorted my foggy vision.

My newfound aides guided me through another set of double doors, and we were in a small steam room with slotted wooden tiers. Immediately to the right was a pile of huge towels. I wrapped one around me and the feel of it was magnificent, like crushed velvet. After some small discussion, the women apparently decided where I should be shelved—out of harm's way and within their joint fields of vision. I wound up on the third of five tiers, banked above and below by the bodies of my comrades. Once that protective strategy was in operation, the message was that we should all relax. This dictum they conveyed by popping up into a semisitting posture, then each in turn feigning instant collapse with varying degrees of credibility.

I found myself laughing hard and loud. This delighted the women who were clearly pleased that somehow the whole affair had turned into a hyggelig (cozy) afternoon—a state of being that is superior to euphoria and more valued by the Danes than high adventure.

With the heat of the room and the heat of my wounds I felt a pleasant numbing of consciousness. The last thing I remembered was the hyggelig hiss of temperate steam.

I awoke to find the room deserted except for a woman stretched out above me and another standing below me. My eyes opened to their intent gaze and I scrambled to my feet. On the wall a recessed clock with illuminated red hands read exactly four o'clock. "Four o'clock!" I said. Thor was punctual. He'd be waiting outside.

I tucked my towel around me and headed in full flight down the wide treads of the steam room. Remembering my gracious and enduring guardian angels, I turned around and went back and thanked each, solemnly shaking hands and enunciating the requisite "Farvel, farvel!" Then I took to the stairs again. The double doors through which we had entered would not budge. I raised my knuckles to pound and my friends were beside me again. "No, No! You may not!" They tugged me to another set of doors in the opposing wall.

I flung them open to find a swimming pool in which a half-dozen women were motionlessly emerged, only their bare

shoulders visible, enjoying the water. Warm water! I could see
the steam rising from it in blue-white wisps. A pool. Of course.
My God! I had almost walked out of there without that final,
glorious swish through abundant water.

"Yes! yes!" I said jubilantly.

Beside us was a stainless steel cart, piled high with steam-
room towels. I added mine. As my toes gripped the side of the
pool I was aware of my friends absorbed in the careful folding
of their discarded towels. I had simply dumped mine, forever
the ugly American. I dove and there was the elegant rush of warm
water. Intuitively I had dived shallowly. And that proved
fortunate. Before my hips hit the water, my open eyes could see
the configuration of tiles inches away from my nose, and I
abruptly cut the downward motion of my body. The momentum
carried me half the length of the pool.

As I surfaced I rolled over on my back to look behind me. There
stood the bathers, fully erect now, their knees visible over the
water line. At the far end of the pool, where I had soared so
wantonly into space, my two friends stood etched motionlessly
in stark terror like a Picasso canvas from his blue period, their
faces stunned and uncomprehending.

I stood up abruptly, feeling the water pull away from my body,
and smiled so that my friends might know I was unbloodied and
intact and so that the other occupants might resume their soaking
positions secure in the knowledge there would be no repetition
of the attack. As I climbed the two small steps that led out of
the pool, my two friends raced to my side. One blessed herself,
and the other put both hands to her heart to indicate the
expectation of an imminent attack. I conveyed my contrite state.
"I am fine. Just fine," I assured them.

Beyond them I suddenly observed a second and smaller pool.
It was nevertheless sizable, and all of a sudden I was struck with
a very obvious way in which I might indicate my reformed
approach to the bath. I would show them that I knew how to
behave decorously, as I availed myself of this, the obvious final
rinse.

This pool was empty and I wondered how many of the more
fainthearted I had driven from it by my exhibition. Fixing my
gaze on my friends' still saucer-wide eyes, I moved swiftly down
the two tiled treads, ready to assume the appropriate crouch

beneath its warm surface. "See!" I said, addressing the women once again. I took a third purposeful step into the pool and my body plunged down and down through ice water as I experienced a sharp constriction of my breath and a rigidity of chest and legs. When at last my toes touched the glacially cold bottom, I was able with a spasmodic push to force myself upward again, my hands shaping a channel through the freezing water. I could see above me a pale blue circle of light through which I must surface.

I cut through the water line like a flying fish, with a long-held shriek that emptied the warm pool of bodies and brought attendants through exits and entrances.

"You mean to tell me," said Thor later, "that you dove into the cold tank?"

"I didn't dive," I told him. "I walked in. That is, I walked until I fell in."

"I still don't know why you were fooling around with the cold tank at all," he said. "Even the Danes give that a wide berth. Except for some masochistic nuts."

We had left the bathhouse at a quarter to five. I had reached the rendezvous point under the solicitous escort of Hilde, an attendant. Once outside she pressed into my hand a free pass to "one private bath," and in an ardent but brief review of the afternoon clearly tried to bring home to Thor the desirability of shepherding me out of the public sector.

We piled into the VW. "I'll bet you feel pretty clean, though," Thor said good-naturedly. He had never sounded more Danish. I thought of the Danish fairy tales, of Hans Christian Andersen's happy penchant for horror stories. If I had *drowned* in the ice tank, the consensus would have been that I had died content — having known the great joy of the hot tank. Thor's conviction that, all things said and done, I had had a great time, was not improving my mood.

"How much steam did you take?" I asked, shifting the discussion.

"Oh, no steam," he said casually. "I didn't get the deluxe ticket. I just had a long hot soak. Do you know those tubs are almost six feet long?"

I looked at him.

"You had a bath, a *regular* bath, didn't you?"

He turned and gave me a little pat on the knee as the car moved into the major stream of traffic.

"I didn't mind," he said grandly.

We were going to be late picking up Katie. There was no time for a cup of hot coffee. When we got home I headed for the cupboard and poured myself a shot of aquavit, that fiery Danish brandy. As a matter of fact, I had two.

Thor looked at me in amazement.

"Don't ask!" I said, and went to pick up Katie over at the Jensens'.

5

Social Networking
The Queen's Lace Caper

Throughout our residence on Amager Island, fieldwork involved a sustained kind of physical, as well as intellectual, monitoring. In later years, our memories of the island were triggered as often through sensory links as through remnants of the slow cognitive bonding that we so gropingly developed over the year of our life there.

Unlike our overeager brains, our senses remained resistant and disbelieving in the face of Taarnby's new reality. They clung persistently to a learned logic about the proper sources of bodily comfort. We were never oblivious to the smell of the sea, with its sinister message of power over us, imbuing our small cottage, even in summer, with the dire promise of impending cold. Unprepared taste buds, programmed for different foods, scorned all efforts—mine especially—to adapt to the enjoyment of eel or beer soup. The realization that for twelve months I should be separated from green salads gave a greater reality to the perception of time than the awesome challenge of what we, as anthropologists, had to accomplish within that time. Even my nose resisted odors that, I was later to understand, distinguish villages everywhere and become as encoded and subliminally distinctive of a particular community as a DNA profile of a person.

I was unprepared for the advantage of our six-year-old's presence and for the dimensions of life in Taarnby that were opened or clarified for us through her.

Katie took to disappearing after school and on weekends. The village, with its narrow cobbled streets and the virtual absence of automobile traffic, was safe enough, but I didn't want her popping into houses uninvited or mooching Danish food, of which she was becoming inordinately fond. She could down a pickled herring with more gusto than a chocolate bar. Besides, it was harrowing not knowing where she was.

I would take to the streets. Usually the first or second woman I met had a report of sorts for me — where she was last seen, with whom, and in what state of dress or undress. Katie would be embarrassed and distressed to receive prompt word that she was wanted at home. She would return, pushing at the heavy door, midway in a sullen complaint.

I encouraged her to bring children home. And she did, but infrequently at first.

"It isn't easy," Katie said one day when I heard scuffling and opened the door to find her dragging an unwilling but polite little boy behind her. "I promised him a chocolate cupcake and a red pencil."

Franz was a charmer, blond and handsome with that fragile, fine-boned face of little boys, the jawline still emerging, like a worked piece of sculpture very near completion. Now, in July, Franz wore the brief shorts which, except in the dead of winter, Danish boys wear regardless of weather, just as girls delight in light cotton dresses that billow out behind their bicycles as they pump along the harbor roads.

Since it was lunchtime, I gave them each a peanut butter sandwich, along with the promised chocolate cupcake and red pencil. Peanut butter was unknown in the village, and Franz had a hard time with it, the more because its exact nature was obscured by a second, or top, piece of bread — also an unknown in a community where children's lunch boxes had sliding trays to accommodate the open-faced smørrebrød. I think too that Franz must have heard something of the perils of food produced at the hands of "the American lady," as I was now widely identified.

But Katie, a born authoritarian, who had been dubbed by the villagers "the little general," had the situation under control. "Eat it, you'll like it," she said. "We don't give this to just anyone you know." All in proper singsongy Danish. I was wildly jealous of her swiftly growing mastery of the language.

The level of intimidation was appropriate, as was the privileged-food reference. Franz lifted the sandwich. I averted my eyes. The tension was almost more than I could bear. Child-poisoner would be more than any reputation could withstand. However, when I returned from the kitchen with two glasses of orange soda (special treat), Franz was wiping his mouth, his eyes glazed. His plate was empty.

"You see, I told you," Katie was saying.

Franz was looking at me expectantly, and I went out and made him another sandwich.

The next day Katie returned from kindergarten a pied piper, with Franz and three more children in tow. That wiped out the remaining peanut butter, but it was worth it. I had, in the process, pieced together the village ethic on the care and feeding of children.

When not in school, youngsters are in and out of houses all day long. They are fed wherever they happen to be, at noontime or snack time, which in Denmark is anytime. The day after my soup-and-sandwich session Katie thrust one foot and her head through the front door to announce, "I'm having potatoes and gravy at Tante Tove's!" And she was gone.

And so it went. Hospitality extended beyond food. Katie learned to knit in one home, to do cross-stitching at another, to paint furniture in a third, and was to do holiday baking in a half-dozen kitchens.

Each youngster had a curfew. Jane (pronounced 'Ya-noo' in Danish) would walk in at 9:00 A.M. on a weekend, remove her sweater, and cheerily state: "I have to be home at 6:00 P.M." It was thoroughly alarming at first. I envisaged nine-hour visits and the challenge of unrelieved entertainment. But the practice was simply standard village procedure. Children roamed placidly from house to house, grazing for food and diversion, but were to be returned punctually (by the last hostess of the day) to their own cottages at the appointed hour.

In all of this two factors remained constant. First, the abundant goodwill for which Denmark is famous stems from the realization that, whatever the provocations or petty trials of daily life, nurturance is close at hand.

"As a national character study," Thor advised me, "Denmark remains at an oral stage of fixation. Danes can handle any crisis with equanimity, with the exception of a threat, real or imagined, to their clear access to food." I could now, with hindsight (recurrent in fieldwork), recognize the appalling dimensions of my abortive role as cook.

In Taarnby, a second factor was linked to the immediacy of survival needs in this island community. Tiny, windswept, in many ways more a part of the sea than of the land, simply to endure, Taarnby depended on the highly developed social network into which Katie had been so swiftly admitted. Historically this network had been created by its pilots, sailors, and fishermen. From the tiny glassed-in turrets which projected like jeweled treetops, pilot families watched through telescopes for ships entering the Øresund from the Baltic Sea or the Kattegat, ready for the bell from the harbor that would bring men to the pilot boat or salvage ship in a system of rotation of craft and crew.

When maritime crews were active, seamen stalked the harbor jetties, spreading the news on cargo and tides and sailing dates. From gathering places along the beach where nets were dried and gear repaired, fishermen relayed information on where the cod were last sighted or where an errant school of herring had suddenly appeared.

Within their own world, the women of the village were no less efficient. At the period of our residence, theirs was a network which, more than the declining sea world of the men, continued to shape village life. My friend Tove called my attention to the "street mirrors" affixed outside the windows of most houses like the rearview mirror on an automobile.

"A woman can sit and knit, shell nuts, sort rice, and not miss a trick," she said. "Is Olga still seeing young Lars? Did Mogens's wife finally let him invest in a new overcoat? Is Zibrantsen still lapping up beers at the tavern while his wife visits her cousin? The women know what's happening before people's families do."

Neighbors faced each other across roads that were often too narrow for a large car to pass. "In the late afternoon you can see them, the old ladies in their dark dresses and shawls, even in the dead of winter, making their appointed rounds to visit other grandmothers who man street mirrors beyond their territory," Tove noted. A kind of archgrandmother in black mentally logged entries from the reporting staff within her domain. This information was then dispersed outward and downward in the hierarchy.

Life in Taarnby was relentlessly and in all seasons life in a goldfish bowl. Thus Thor knew before I reached home that I had gone to Fru Falster's home beauty parlor to have my hair washed. "Word has it you're vain," he said.

"Word does?" I said, somewhat undone by this response to my struggle for a clean head.

"Actually I was asked if all American women spent so much for pretty hair!"

"Oh God."

He had picked up this captivating commentary at the harbor— from the wife of a fisherman who had come with her husband's lunch pail. Their cottage, along the rim of the seawall, was as remote as one could get from the tiny house in which Fru Falster had installed, at shocking cost, hot water and an eighteen-inch sink.

What the street mirrors missed, the children of the village provided. They did this, for the most part, virtuously and unwittingly. But their clear access to all homes made them an irresistible source of information. In Taarnby they were calculatedly pumped for news by an attentive and competitive adult relay system.

Sometimes the system had mixed dividends. Katie had her skinned knee cleaned and dressed before she could get her new scooter home to tell me about the accident. Of course by then she had imparted to her attentive nurse the source of the scooter (a prestigious Copenhagen store) and the donor (immediately relayed through the system as a wealthy American grandmother). As to its price, Katie, to the amazement of her examiner, was uninformed.

Housewives revelled in reputations of being "the first to know," a distinction that required time, talent, and clout. Fru Strunge, the chief pilot's wife, whose unusually spacious cottage faced ours, was one such woman. And one morning she took on the challenge of determining what mission was taking Thor and me out of Taarnby for the entire day while Katie partied at Anna Møller-Pedersen's.

I should have known that this stretch of undocumented, and perhaps undocumentable, time would be intolerable. We had no sooner gotten Katie off than there was a knock on the door. Thor and I exchanged pained glances. We had decided to use the day for a ferryboat ride to Sweden, which I had never visited. "A whole day to call our own," Thor had said. "It's going to be great." Free-floating togetherness. There was in his eyes the anticipation of hours of privacy and the renewed enjoyment of just being together. We had stored away much of that enjoyment in the enthusiasms of fieldwork. It was time for a break.

The boat for Sweden left from an ancient slip on Denmark's mainland, and if we were to make the last morning ferry we had precious little time to spare. But now, in walked Fru Strunge's granddaughter.

"I should greet you from my grandmother," she said with stock formality. "She asks that you stop by her house before getting away."

No explanation, of course, as to just how her grandmother knew we were "getting away." To my consternation I heard Thor tell her to relay the message that we would be right along. My mouth went dry with apprehension. The girl left, and when he saw my face, Thor put his arms around me. He laughed consolingly.

"Whatever it is, we'll only stay a minute. It won't do any good to offend the woman." He was right, of course.

"Just don't sit down," I said, uncomforted. "Just don't sit down."

"I won't sit down," he promised. And then, inspired, "Let's keep our coats on."

"And under no circumstances take them off," I added. "What she wants is to find out where we're going. And I'm damned if I'm going to tell her. This village is going to have to learn that *some* things are our own business."

"It might be simpler just to tell the woman."

"No way!" I said firmly.

In later years, with the experience of other villages behind us, I would come to appreciate that this need to know was widely characteristic of the intimate nature of village life and necessarily endured wherever our fieldwork took us. But on this occasion in Taarnby, I felt indignation mounting in me and along with it a zeal for silence in the face of this beyond-the-pale ferreting for information.

"There will," I assured Thor, "be no news for the network on the Andersons' sortie. Agreed?" I put my hand out and we shook on it.

"Agreed!"

We would simply tell Fru Strunge we had to be on our way. No elaborations. Fast in, fast out, and off to Sweden.

The ferry to Sweden would move us into the full sweep of arctic winds, so we had armloads of garments we intended to toss into the car, which we would take on the ferry. We decided to get into our greatcoats and caps with earflaps—the better to look ready for the road. By the time I had stuffed the passports and papers into my purse and rounded up the scarves and sunglasses, my forehead was headed in perspiration. Indoors the knitted fibers smelled faintly of the semiprocessed animal hair whose natural oils contributed to their singular warmth.

If we looked unusual, Fru Strunge gave no hint of it. She stood in the doorway in the dark cotton skirt, bright long-sleeved blouse, and generous print apron that were almost a village uniform. The house was already fragrant with the smell of baking. I wondered idly if she was contributing to the Møller-Pedersen's birthday party fare.

Fru Strunge was given to unrelieved smiling. She was smiling now as, talking all the way, she led us to her parlor. "Ah! So good of you to come. And such a lovely morning. But one is never sure how long the sun will hold with the wind coming out of the sound. However, my husband tells me, 'Be grateful when the day is warm and do not ask how long the warmth will last!'"

We had to follow or allow her to find herself talking to herself. My eyes met Thor's. She had outmaneuvered us in our clear intent to remain fixed in the doorway. We refused her offer to take our coats. In that we were firm.

The Strunge house offered an unobstructed view of the sound, and through the skylight the unusual morning sun flooded the small, plump sofas, which faced one another across a polished table, set now with a shimmering decanter and a plate full of the Queen's Lace cookies that were Fru Strunge's culinary signature.

At the sight of them Thor promptly sat down. Later he insisted that he too was in shock, that he too saw the enormity of the challenge ahead of us. But I think it was simply the Danish food reflex in action. In any case, I felt betrayed as he launched into the obligatory stream of Danish compliments on the charming room, lovely cookies, and thoughtfulness of our hostess. I could see that morning ferry pulling out of the slip without us. What ensued I still have difficulty reconstructing. Nor do I know by what cognitive route I decided upon the course of action I took. But a decision did leap to mind and fix itself there.

Fru Strunge had seated herself next to Thor, waiting for me to settle. I moved swiftly to the other sofa and eased myself to its edge. In front of me was a small pile of heirloom plates and a studious distribution of tiny napkins with crocheted edges. Thor and Fru Strunge were still in the preliminaries of civilities that for five minutes precede and follow any joint intake of food by Danes. Reconfirmed in my decision, I nudged Fru Strunge, handed her a plate and a napkin, and then, stretching across the table placed a plate and napkin on Thor's knee. His eyes widened in astonishment and a brief spasm threatened Fru Strunge's happy countenance.

"There is wine," she said, compelled now to do something about the glasses.

"Sweet vermouth," I said, transfixed at the first sip. It was a setback. I didn't know what I could do with a decanter of sweet vermouth, but there was to be no turning back.

The plate of cookies, fragrant and warm, began its slow circulation. Thor commented for the third time on their fragile beauty.

"You are surely Taarnby's finest cook, Fru Strunge," he said. His panic over my usurpation of the hostess role had provoked a lavish line of diverting praise. Fru Strunge blushed happily.

The cookies *were* magnificent. Their simple appearance belied, I knew, the great skill involved in their preparation. Slender, curved ovals, paper-thin in their near transparency, they needed to be baked without browning and curved without breaking when taken hot from the oven. The sugar coating must achieve the patina of fine silver and was hellish to apply. "I have made only a half batch," said Fru Strunge. "I wanted them to be warm so that you might start off your trip with something protective in your stomach.''

Your trip was duly emphasized. Fru Strunge was bent on the extraction of information. It was the end of the last flickering of remorse as to what I must do.

"I, for one, do not intend to resist them,'' I said. And I delicately slid three cookies onto my plate from the airborne position in which Fru Strunge still held the serving platter. I was deep into mental arithmetic on the number represented in "half a batch.'' Probably little more than what lay before us. I gave a rough count, figuring by sets of three. Fifteen cookies. I looked at the loquacious, probing Fru Strunge and the acquiescent Thor and knew full well where the challenge lay.

I began now to eat and drink in earnest. I knew we should never get out until the plate and the decanter were empty. Eventually I developed a kind of rhythm. I had begun with two bites of cookie and a sip of wine, but the wine volume lagged. That could constitute a threat of major magnitude. If we got lopsided, out of cookies but not out of wine, Fru Strunge would—under the rules—have to dash out to her kitchen and replenish the bakery end of it. That could lead to more wine and we'd be into the usual pattern of uninterruptible eating.

I shifted the tempo: a bite of cookie, two sips of wine. Thor, early during our stay in the village, had announced a chronic and obscure minor stomach disorder that forbade anything but the most minimal intake of sweets and alcohol. Tactically, it was brilliant. I could not fault him for that. But it did place a monumental burden on me in that it would have been quite unthinkable for the two of us to be relatively unfeedable.

But now Thor's nerve was leaving him. Fru Strunge's initial pleasure in my "delight" over the "little meal" had shifted to some confusion about my single-minded absorption in it. Thor diverted the decanter to his glass (a bold move in itself) and soon was busy on the cookies, his head lowered, his eyes poised, I knew, for the moment when he might rivet them onto mine.

And then it happened, the last cookie and only a faint amber glow caught by the sun in the bottom of the decanter. Fru Strunge, a large-framed woman, put out her hand to the arm of the sofa, and I recognized the gesture, that first pulling together that would have her on her feet, empty platter in hand on her way to the kitchen. I was ready for her, my hand on her shoulder. "Oh please, thank you, nothing more. We are planning to eat breakfast on the road." I looked at Thor.

"Breakfast on the road," he said, standing.

I could feel the upward thrust of her body against my hand, but she was still too deep into the sofa cushions. And then, in the ritualized village format of farewell, I added, "Thank you for the food. It was lovely and really much too much."

But in the car, as we sped across the inlet and toward Copenhagen, Thor, with vigorous chastisement, told me that the words actually came out, "Thank you for the snack. It was lovely and almost enough." His monologue went on for some twenty miles of intense driving. "God knows what that woman thinks of us," he said rhetorically for the second time.

"She thinks that you are a fabulous man married to a complete dolt," I said. "But that can scarcely have come as a revelation." I was boundlessly happy.

"Can you imagine what she will have fed into the network?" Thor asked.

"That her Queen's Lace were devoured by the Americans faster and more appreciatively than any pastry a Taarnby housewife could hope to produce," I replied. "Why she's probably walking the news around herself!"

"Not really."

"Really," I said. "Our visit will go down in local history, and the historical society will put a plaque in her kitchen."

I drove. Thor hated European roads. We took off our coats and hats and rolled down the windows. The air was magnificent on our steaming bodies, although my head ached, and the wine lay in my stomach like four vanilla milk shakes.

We were jubilant when the ancient pier came into sight on the far side of Copenhagen's coastline, and the ferry was there, blasting sounds of imminent departure. We had made it. Something suddenly occurred to me, and I yelled triumphantly across the sound to Sweden and the world, "And they haven't the damnedest idea where we've gone!"

We got on board, the last car to be admitted. On deck we were shepherded out of the car and topside. At the rail Thor put his arms around me as we watched the wide wake of the blunt-sterned ferryboat. Denmark receded slowly from view. I felt

Thor's body convulse with laughter. "You *were* dreadful," he said, but when he looked at me the words were warm with affection.

"I know," I said penitently. "I'd have locked her in the kitchen to get out of there."

"I rather wish you'd thought of that first."

The engines began to pick up speed, and the rhythmic throbbing filtered through the ship, sending vibrations along my legs and into my vermouth-filled stomach. "Thor," I said, leaning heavily against him.

"What is it, honey?"

"I think I'm about to pay for my sins."

And he moved me gingerly but swiftly to the rail.

6

Acquiring Status
A New Villager

T ogether we had begun to identify dimensions of village life that were being reshaped by change: everything from social organization to sexual behavior. We were hugely helped by some pertinent local histories of the area that Thor managed to acquire and translate.

Our days were becoming more productive. Thor and I put together a questionnaire exploring the effect upon family life of the accelerating demise of the maritime base of Taarnby's economy. We were interested as well in the emerging centrality of Copenhagen, as sons and daughters of many families turned from the sea to the nearby capital for work and for socializing.

We sought out members of the diminishing numbers of families of pilots, ships' captains, and maritime officers. In Taarnby, by the time a man had achieved the work experience and passed the examinations required for pilot or ship's captain, he was mature. He could look back on a kaleidoscope of change. His wife, too, was generally old enough to provide depth of insight into former life styles and the values that had shaped them. In households where these couples had a surviving parent, reconstruction of once-dominant mores could be pushed into the vivid script of Taarnby's past maritime zenith. We talked with children and grandchildren of residents. Through the reconstruction of assorted life spans a broad canvas of history had begun to take vibrant shape.

47

In all we interviewed forty-one women, twenty-two men, and fifteen children. Transcriptions of notes devoured hours. If an interview went one hour, at least two hours were required to get the data onto cards.

As we ventured into the kind of in-depth interviewing that went beyond questionnaire items and that sometimes extended into several protracted sessions, men initially proved more comfortable with Thor than with me. Part of it was Thor's level of language proficiency. As the months progressed, I acquired more male informants.

Fishermen took a dim view of having women aboard their boats, even though husband-and-wife teams had been common on the small craft. Nevertheless, from the beginning of our fieldwork, getting out into the open sound on one of the boats seemed to me a critical adventure. Once, determinedly, I had succeeded in having that experience (and returning, had seen Taarnby reappear like the haven it must have represented for generations of seamen), I did not challenge the conviction of many of the men that a woman aboard was bad luck.

An important function of the interviewing was that these sessions allowed informants the opportunity to ask questions of us. What they most sought to comprehend was what on earth had brought us as strangers to live in this place on the globe. What possible creditable motive—they needed to know—could have generated our interest in small Taarnby?

Responding to these concerns was my introduction to what would become a ritual in the field: establishment of some framework within which work as an anthropologist can be accepted, if not fully understood. The idea that I had accompanied Thor to Taarnby with the limited intent of fulfilling wifely and motherly obligations never took substantial hold. My initial shabby performance as cook and housekeeper may have contributed to this conviction. When my activities ventured beyond innocuous involvement in daily life to pointed questioning (unrelated to housekeeping), there was more relief than concern among the women. As Fru Wikman, the bakery lady, told me pridefully, "I knew you were up to something."

I grew careful always to preface a professional contact with an unhurried statement as to what I would be interested in learning and why. And I would attempt some explanation of why the information which I lacked but they were privileged to possess—about village organizations or funeral rites or marital expectations—would further the goals of our study.

The villagers knew that Thor had a doctorate. In this very literate country, that fact alone had commendable associations. In formal address and introductions he was Herr Doktor Anderson. My less definable (predoctoral) status invited more qualified approval. With the doctorate, I would have been Doktor Fru Anderson. Nevertheless, as Tove told me one afternoon, "People really are pleased to know what it is you're good at."

Over the year perhaps a half-dozen villagers—I doubt that there were more—ceased to wonder what exactly compelled us to do whatever it was we did. Men and women continued to regard our work rather like some absorbing avocation. The woman who ran the dairy-products shop and who was crazy about Katie, into whose hands she always thrust a stubby square of cheese on a stick (Taarnby's equivalent of a lollipop), told me that a man who collected butterflies came every summer, as did a man who searched the beaches for "historical" things washed up from old wrecks. Then she would smile benignly to let me know that Thor and I were in good company.

I continued to do many of the things that engaged other women of the village. We had succeeded, however, in persuading our neighbor, Fru Odstadt, to do some part-time housekeeping for us. That arrangement liberated me further. Thor was always visible in Taarnby's streets, involved largely with the men and with men's work. (Neither the men nor the women of Taarnby would have appreciated his busying himself too much in my obvious household responsibilities.) Katie's school schedule and mealtimes anchored our days and allayed whatever community concerns periodically surfaced about us. Obviously and unqualifiedly we were a family among families, a claim to membership in the community that was soon to be further reinforced.

September came and I was four months pregnant. I unpacked the maternity wardrobe I had used when I was pregnant with Katie, determined to invest as little as possible of our limited money on additions to it.

Thor was worried. "You'll never get through a Danish winter in those wash-and-wear things," he said.

I knew he was right, that I would have to do some imaginative dressing if I were to make it to February when the baby was due. I was heartened by the Danish predilection for portable accessories and the layering of clothes.

As we moved into October the sun lost its vigor. "It's a Swedish sun," Fru Odstadt told me, imbuing it with the transient goodwill Danes like to associate with their wealthier neighbors. Children were stuffed into sweaters, though young boys still clung to shorts that barely reached the upper thigh.

There began that endless pulling on and off of clothes, and the double rows of great metal hooks in our small entry hall were always overflowing. I came to know the jerky maneuvering which meant that some elusive sleeve had slid up under an armpit and needed to be coaxed down. I learned to pull a child's sweater over the head so as not to leave a lacerated ear. A few children were into the jogging suits which precede the snow wear of dead winter.

"Watch the wind," Herr Strunge told me with pilot wisdom. "When it shifts in the Øresund, funneling in from the northwest, there's worsening weather ahead. It can hit you like a body blow."

A kind of panic seized me the first time I felt that wind on my exposed forehead, painful and direct as a laser beam. The milkman began leaving our bottles anchored in metal stands, for the arctic blasts could dash full containers against the garden wall.

Already the sun was withdrawing to a narrowing band of light that would soon trace a 360 degree circle of apricot between the dark earth and a sky of perpetual twilight. Outdoors our breath came in rhythmic clouds of white vapor.

"I hope we can keep this coke-hungry *kakkelovn* going all winter," Thor said, shaking his head with a visible dearth of optimism. And dark Jack London stories of death in the Yukon came suddenly to mind.

Whatever reservations I had about sartorial compromises to the cold vanished. I studied what the women wore with voracious interest. When visiting, they retreated at once to inner rooms and there left mountains of woolens behind them.

"What is all that stuff?" I asked Tove, always my resource person, one day in her cottage. "What's that little round thing like a doughnut?"

"A doughnut?"

"Knitted. They wear them like bracelets."

"Ah. A *muffedise*," said Tove. "It traps any air that finds its way between your gloves and where your sweater begins. A kind of wind seal. Very cozy."

I said, "Every bed has a pile of slacks on it."

"They're not really slacks," Tove corrected. "It's a kind of loose outdoor long john. Not very pretty, but warm. You put them on to travel from place to place. Nobody would dream of sitting around in them. You pull them off as soon as you get indoors. You can buy them at Schroeder's. I may even have a few extra you can use."

Most of these garments ranged on a monochromatic scale from beige to the browny-black produced by the constant washing and bleeding of dark clothes.

In the days that followed I piled everything on and under, achieving the rotund look of a fuzzy Kewpie doll. I invented layers, including a collar version of the *muffedise*. A suit of Thor's cashmere-soft long underwear shrank alarmingly, and I promptly claimed it, ignoring his veiled suggestion of prior intent. With the buttons removed and plaid ribbons substituted, I had maternity lingerie.

Katie thrived. Her late August birthday had brought an avalanche of fancy winter wear from grandparents, and she cut an elegant figure in the village. Thor had a limited but impressive wardrobe from previous visits. And if my dowdiness was viewed as an anomaly—all Americans are wealthy—I was saved from permanent stigma when my pregnant condition finally became apparent.

The network spread this startling development with its usual efficiency. "The American Lady is going to have a villager!" For that was the way it translated. *A villager*. Awesome news of the first order. In Taarnby the only way one could acquire village status was to be *born* in the village.

"Not even the widow Ulla, who came here sixty years ago a bride and had seven children in Taarnby, is considered a villager," Tove told me. "Her children, yes; Widow Ulla, no."

"Lars Skjern, who was delivered six miles away in Store Astrup, where his mother had gone to buy hams and cheeses, forfeited his claim," Fru Strunge felt compelled to tell me.

"True," Tove reiterated. "And it's very painful for the family, since Store Astrup is a village of farmers, not seamen." In this community where the sea alone bred freedom of body and spirit, identification with the land was denigrating.

Being a villager meant coming into the world optimally fit for the rugged existence the sea exacted from those who lived on or beside it. And the pride of Taarnby was now invested in the well-being of this prospective new addition. Solicitousness for my welfare reached smothering proportions, as a kind of "save the child" panic swept the community. The concerns of the women were veiled only thinly, if at all. I was too small, too thin, too narrow of hip. It was common knowledge that American women did not nurse their children.

"They don't, do they?" asked Fru Nysgaard one afternoon, clearly commissioned to confirm this tenet.

"The consensus is that you'll have no milk even if you try," Tove reported.

I was far too athletic, given my condition. And I had been observed racing about the treacherous cobblestones in shoes with two-inch heels. No good would come of it.

In the guise of a social visit, an "inspection team" went over our house, and Fru Molsted feigned a seizure when she saw what she called its "ancient" condition and learned that I was still climbing from the kitchen to our upstairs bedroom on what was actually a fixed ladder. "And there are only three walls up there!" she cried. "Without so much as a railing to protect you from sure death on the tiles below."

The tiles below — which was actually an expanse of cement — immediately took on a menacing dimension I had never before considered. We had thought the ladder to be one of the more romantic aspects of the cottage, along with the recessed beds — small, medium, and large — like something out of Goldilocks — with doors that promised instant claustrophobia for anyone brave enough to close them against the night chill.

Herr Ringe, postman and carpenter, arrived one evening after work. "I have been instructed to take care of the windows," he announced, grinning sheepishly, "by my wife." He caulked the areas around the rotted sills where shrinkage and weather had shifted their alignment with the frames. And he returned the next night, with profuse excuses for the inconvenience, and installed a half-dozen new panes to replace those that wobbled. Payment in money was out of the question, and we found ourselves pressed to find opportunities to compensate our attentive neighbors in some way.

If we had chafed previously at the invasion of our privacy, we were now reduced to the most taxing subterfuges to insure some time alone together. Every day seemed to bring to some family the realization that we were insufficiently briefed on something, and a visit was in order.

In my role as anthropologist, the development was cause for delight. The resistance with which a number of my inquiries had been met vanished, dissolved in a surfeit of goodwill that had informants virtually lining up for discussions of anything from fishing rights and feuds to data for a proposed chapter on sexual behavior (information about which is generally more or less opportunely gathered or collected in a fail-safe scheduling late in the fieldwork).

The occasional sorties that Thor and I now made into Copenhagen were associated by the villagers with our research needs and access to documents housed in the capital. Our work did bring us into the city to complete a demographic profile of the area and to confer with specialists at the University of Copenhagen. But what they did not know—not even Tove—was that, in addition, these excursions allowed me to keep appointments with a Copenhagen obstetrician. Katie had been delivered after a near-Caesarian section, and Thor and I were now ambivalent about having the baby delivered by the village midwife.

In Denmark midwifery is an old and respected practice, and the young midwives of today are scrupulously trained and licensed. Delivery at the Royal Hospital in Copenhagen, to which my obstetrician was attached, was limited to cases where difficulty was anticipated or developed during labor. In Taarnby, it was a rare circumstance that found an experienced midwife needing to bring in a physician. To unleash for networking this testimony of the cowardice of the American woman and the ignominy of robbing our unborn child of the right to villager status would be folly.

In December I was still vacillating about what course to take: stand my ground in the hallowed tradition of anthropology or take the more secure course and head for Copenhagen as soon as I went into labor. The village midwife, whom I had met, was of advanced and indeterminate age and among the most dolorous of women. With a penchant for brevity which she reputedly extended to the labor bed, she was said to sit soundlessly beside her charge except for the periodic rejoinder that, "There, there, it will get worse!"

Chance stepped in, and Katie developed *impetigo*. I fled with her to Dr. Lars's office and joined the perpetual queue of women and children, and the occasional man, who ordered themselves in line in the waiting room chairs. Katie was given an ointment and was sent to play with Dr. Lars's granddaughter while I told him candidly of my dilemma.

"I think your decision to keep both options open is an ideal one," he said. "If February is as harsh as usual, you may well find yourself snowbound with no alternative in any case." It would be wise, he told me, to anticipate the possibility of a village child.

"And remember," he added smiling, "no part of the village is more than ten minutes from my door. One way or another you can be sure the country has the resources to bring one more Dane into the world."

In brief, the dimensions of my faintheartedness were appreciated even by Dr. Lars. "And," he added, "if you ask old Anna, the whaler's wife, she will tell you whether it will be a fine son or a fine daughter."

On the 20th of January, Sarah was born at the Royal Hospital in Copenhagen, where I was prepared for a Caesarian section by Dr. Brandstrup, the royal obstetrician, who happened to be in the building at the time of our midnight arrival. Thor had made the agonizingly slow ride between snowstorms along deserted roads banked with deep drifts. Old Anna had been right about the sex of the child, having predicted a girl on the basis of the way I slept (girls like the left, or heart, side, forcing the mother to favor that side when at rest), and my relative lack of food cravings during pregnancy (boys are thought to make assertive demands).

The Danish hospital system was a joy. During the nine days of my confinement, Sarah never left my side except for a 2:00

A.M. bottle-feeding in the hospital nursery to afford me uninterrupted sleep. She lay next to me in a small basket-crib the height of my bed. I could touch her and talk to her and lift her to me whenever I chose.

There were twelve new mothers on the floor, a winter record, and from time to time, while Sarah slept, I interviewed them and administered a questionnaire on child-rearing practices and on the mother's expectations for her son or daughter. In later months, we would use these data comparatively in a survey of Taarnby mothers.

I was expected to nurse Sarah, and all the resources of the hospital were geared to assuring a bountiful supply of milk. Mothers were expected to drink liberally of apple and orange soda water and of a dark malt beer. It was odd to look around the four-bed ward with starched white curtains, carefully tucked bed linens, and gleaming floors buffed each day with lamb's wool, and catch the sunlight bounce off a bottle of Tuborg's best. Or watch the nurse whisk in with a tray of eight or ten bottles and check the empties, reminding me, more often than not, that I was not "keeping up."

"You are privileged as a nursing mother to have one soft-boiled egg daily with breakfast," I was told on the morning after delivery. Eggs are expensive in Denmark and, as in much of Europe, are purchased according to the freshness appropriate for the use of each egg. A Danish housewife would not dream of spending the additional pennies required for a "hen-fresh" egg on one that was to be hard-boiled or merely beaten into a main dish. The top-of-the-line hen-fresh egg is meant to solo.

The enormity of the egg-a-day commitment on the part of the hospital, therefore, did not escape me. To have a nursing mother's tray so adorned constituted public recognition of performance rendered. And I did enjoy the sumptuousness of the escape from the standard coffee-and-roll breakfast.

The one great challenge of the day came at 5:30 A.M., when draperies were still drawn against the falling snow and the few non-nursing mothers lay with another hour of warm sleep yet ahead of them. I would be shaken with gentle firmness until I rose to a sitting position, when before me was pushed a small tray containing an open-faced liverpaste sandwich on dark rye and the day's first bottle of malt beer.

"It will get the milk going," the nurse explained on the first day, when I slid in horror back under the bedclothes. Failure to consume the rations "ordered by the doctor" evoked nonstop remonstrations, loud enough to invite the wrath of those who were spared the ordeal.

One non-nursing mother was, I discovered, covetous of this early-morning windfall. By the third day we had worked out a system whereby I would deliver the tray clandestinely to my appreciative neighbor. Unfortunately, when one morning she fell back to sleep and failed to return the early tray to my table, our little scheme was discovered. The morning nurse, articulate in her disappointment with me, took to sporadic entrances to insure no more transgressions.

It is only fair to acknowledge that these hospital precautions are apparently founded on experience. I developed sufficient milk to become at once something of a celebrity and a heroine. My status as "the American lady" added to the aggrandizement, and I was asked to contribute the extra milk to the clinic for babies with special dietary problems, a service I was happy to render.

Among the dividends was further mobility on the maternity floor. I took advantage of my prolonged stay to expand inquiry about expectations of parents for their children, to the husbands of women I had already talked with on the wards, approaching the men during visiting hours when other relatives absorbed the attention of mother and baby.

When at last Thor drove us all home, Katie was beside herself with the joy of at last having a sister she could hold. My excitement was tempered by the thought I had been pushing into the back of my mind for days. *I was not bringing home "a villager!"*

Sarah, who lay all gold and apricot in my arms, would receive a second-class welcome. The months before delivery during which I had carried her through Taarnby's ancient streets counted for nothing. I had forfeited her right to an inheritance that now seemed unaccountably important.

The waters of the sound reflected a low-slung gray sky and the joy went out of me when I saw the houses pressed together looking cold and alien. What were we all doing here anyway, so far from all the dear familiar things? From grandparents who would not see their new granddaughter for months?

Ours was a corner house, edging the sound. When our Volkswagen made the careful turn into our lane, I saw the red and white Danish flag flying from the top of the mast in our front yard. In Taarnby every house had a flagpole, some affixed to the wall above the street, some centered in the garden where children could help in raising and lowering it. I had never seen ours in use. I didn't even know we owned a flag. When I could pull my eyes away long enough, I saw other flags dipping into the street from various houses the length of Strandlinien. *What day was this?*

Thor parked the car snugly against our house and gingerly took Sarah from me. "Go ahead," he said, opening the shoulder-high gate. The house looked tinier than I had remembered it. A place for elves. A place for Sarah. I opened the door to a scene still etched in my mind.

Streamers of red and white (Denmark's colors) were twisted in graceful arcs across the room, and on the far beam, in that intricate calligraphy that could only have been done by an artist of the old school, were words I could not understand. I turned spontaneously to Thor. He had followed my eyes. "The banner reads: 'Welcome to our adopted daughter!'" he said. "It's Taarnby's way of receiving its own."

Fru Strunge was there, her smile even broader than usual, and Doktor Lars, and the Jensens, Poul my engineer friend and his wife, and Tove, and so many others. The first to embrace me was the midwife, not at all mournful now, though she did find a moment later to ask me if it had been "very bad."

The kitchen was busy. Tove and Fru Jensen circulated mugs of hot chocolate and trays of creamed pastries, jam-filled tarts, and Vienna bread. "And something special for you," said Fru Rasmussen. She gestured significantly toward the carpenter's wife, who, with her ample bulk, had been hiding a tray on a table behind her. She came forward now, ceremoniously extending bottles of Denmark's finest beer.

Fru Strunge made the toast.

"To the health of Taarnby's newest addition and the bountifulness of her American mother."

7

☙◎◗◉◈☙

Identifying
Cultural Themes
A Framework for Data Analysis

F or the anthropologist engaged in first fieldwork, the remembrance of published ethnographies by established professionals is constant and depressing. We had come to Taarnby with a collection of monographs describing cultures that ranged from Australian aborigines and Mexican villagers to a midwestern American community. I read and reread them when I could find the time. As the weeks rolled by, my respect for their authors grew. Orderly and sensitive, these books conveyed what seemed to me inordinate sureness on the part of the anthropologists involved as to the cultural priorities around which to organize a flood of information. Chapters flowed with an unremitting sense of logic and of the inevitability of the authors' eventual conclusions. Page followed page as though programmed from some inbred order—departure from which would be unthinkable. Now, cognitively adrift in Taarnby, it was difficult to remember how critical we, as students, had been of many of these books. Within the reality of our own fieldwork, the simplest published ethnography took on the stature of an epic.

So far as our own research was concerned, order had yet to make itself felt. The nagging suspicion was growing that it should—that by now the one sure framework for our culture change analysis should be apparent.

The expanding collection of five-by-eight-inch cards on which Thor and I were transcribing field notes had resisted a half-dozen efforts toward thematic organization. We needed a framework that would do justice to our growing understanding of the way of life in Taarnby. The importance of enduring cultural themes and of the creeping reorientation of Taarnby's youth from the sea to Copenhagen's job market was now evident, but we were less insightful about how to integrate that knowledge. The revivifying sense of control that followed each consensus gave way to mounting concern when, over and over again, we abandoned one framework to take up yet another. We were, we realized, still far from finding the right way through a burgeoning maze of information.

I am not sure how long neophyte anthropologists cling to the unfortunate conviction—with which they too often enter the field—that there is one right way to bring order to their data and thus dispose them to the right analysis. As though there exists an inevitable mold into which *if all goes as it should*, data will shape themselves with compelling theoretical effect. And if we don't find it, our work will be second-rate. This conviction is crippling. It is never helpful. And it is absurd. The ways in which cumulative insights can legitimately find order and be reported upon effectively and powerfully are numerous. Eventually, as anthropologists we acquire the experience and confidence that allow us to see this. We develop an appreciation of the power of data to speak to us, to provide us with a range of judgments as to how a chapter (or a book) might be organized. We learn that it is all right to abandon any approach without guilt if a particular judgment proves wrong or unworkable.

In Taarnby, I, in particular, was far from these insights. Thor was more sanguine about our eventual success, though still very vulnerable.

Our Danes were complex. Sometimes like warm puppies. Boundlessly friendly, open, and energetic, but self-absorbed. Sublimely content in their own enthusiasms, the most trivial things could engage their interest, and they would not be shaken from them. Thor came home daily with horror stories.

"It's absolutely amazing," he said one afternoon, with no preamble, walking into the house and slamming the door behind him. "Once they get the bit in their teeth there's no stopping them. I'd trade tomorrow with any anthropologist alive for a village of headhunters and communication by sign language."

He pounded the wall in a rare gesture of frustration. I dragged a beer from the cold kitchen tiles (our built-in refrigerator).

"Everything was going great. I'd finally gotten Michelangelo (our name for the local housepainter) away from his cronies long enough to ask some questions. I'll bet that man's been in every house and on every boat in Taarnby. A mine of information! But let him get off the track."

He shook his head, searching for words.

"It's got to be genetic." He waved open palms before him, frustrated. "I asked him to tell me about some of Taarnby's ship families, and he launched into a recounting of the color schemes of ships and houses he has painted over the last ten years, complete with breakdowns of the hues and tints which — 'anyone would testify' — are his first-class, exclusive productions."

He took a swallow of beer. "I must have said 'That's fine, but,' a dozen times, trying to cut him off."

The end came, Thor said, shaking his head with incredulity, only when Michelangelo's wife appeared with a hot-lunch pail. "She moved her arms in front of his face like a semaphore man on the deck of a carrier, and he finally stopped talking, put a napkin around his neck, and reached for his lunch. A total waste of nearly two hours. Two hours!"

He was seated again, head lowered, legs outstretched, in a posture of futility. But then he lifted his chin and burst into laughter. "Not only does he talk nonstop. But 'his ears plug up in the winter,' his wife told me, 'especially the left one' — into which I was pouring my pitiful appeals that we move on to other topics."

But the record was held by "His Honor," a local magistrate whose humble but complex judicial role in the community had been difficult for us to fathom. "I'll take him," Thor had said when we were dividing up the week's informants.

His Honor was bound to have a great deal of experience with the less-than-ideal side of village life, a dimension of daily existence about which the average informant is rarely prone to speak. And so one morning Thor went off, buoyant with hope, his pockets stuffed with notebooks and pencils. "I'm sure I can coax something out of him," he said, kissing me goodbye.

Four hours later Thor returned with glazed eyes. His voice emerged in a zombielike monotone. "His Honor was the pits." I went for the beer.

"From the start of the interview, he assumed the position that nothing he did, absolutely nothing, could be understood unless I grasped the complex forces which shaped his interest in law itself." He fell briefly silent in agonizing reflection. "And so he took me back to his birth—which disappointingly enough was not in Taarnby—to his youthful affinity for the Greek and Latin classics, which he duly named and briefly reviewed, and to his puberty, after which there followed some briefly diverting romances."

"Still no Taarnby," I said.

"No Taarnby," Thor repeated, turning his eyes full upon me. "Every ploy I could come up with to get him onto Taarnby was patiently heard and then summarily dismissed. He all but said 'irrelevant, incompetent, and immaterial.' Then we had the rocky course of his commitment to the law, and finally, when I was afraid I might just commit mayhem, we got to his marriage to his cousin's widow, a woman of Taarnby, and his taking over of someone's law practice, which led, as he put it, 'to his present prominence.'"

"Well, at least you got there. Hellish as it was."

"Oh yes," Thor said. "And with the same breath he observed that it was time for him to keep an appointment about 'a very interesting local matter.'"

When dinner was over, we had a couple of cups of coffee and a larger than usual brandy. Thor had things in perspective again. "Will you see His Honor again?" I asked.

"Tomorrow, if I have the strength."

Nevertheless, life flowed around us with a built-in grace, the quiet rhythm in which the men and women of Taarnby took pride. Like the mariners that many struggled to remain, they enjoyed the studious charting of a given course of action, and this they would pursue with sober and unfaltering dedication.

And in their own good time, with discreet nudging, the villagers helped us to understand the community, its vanishing way of life, and the influences that (twenty years later) would make it a virtual annex of Copenhagen. Michelangelo came round to discussing the people who lived in the houses and boats he painted. His Honor eventually paced himself through some lively tales of the shenanigans of many village families now well-known to us. After eight months of fieldwork, some of the pieces critical to our analysis of change were beginning to fit together.

I was now as involved as Thor in the interviewing. My Danish was imperfect, my vocabulary lopsided, but I had abandoned all hope of any salutary improvement in my accent, and this admission had somehow unleashed in me an extraordinary confidence. I felt I could talk with anyone. It was heady stuff. Thor encouraged me. And in his gracious way he gave not the slightest reminder of how much less a professional I was than he. Nor of my occasionally rocky track record.

We were now more than halfway through our allotted time in the field, and a staggering amount of work remained to be done. Sarah, a relaxed and undemanding baby, nevertheless absorbed time. I did the onerous transcription of my field notes between feedings. My interviews were scheduled for hours when Fru Odstadt could relieve me or when Thor was at home, busy on his own notes. Fru Odstadt's house adjoined ours to the west. Her seaman husband was away for long stretches and she enjoyed Katie and Sarah, on whom she already lavished much attention. On June 15 our landlord would reclaim our cottage, convinced now that if we could live in it, so could "normal people" (as he put it), provided he tended to the plumbing, built real stairs to the second floor, and put in a proper kitchen. So the race was on to finish our fieldwork on schedule and well.

"I think we need a strategy meeting," Thor gravely announced one evening after we had bedded down the children. He got out two glasses and the aquavit which in and of itself signaled, in hallowed Danish fashion, the stature of the occasion. "I've produced a true and final table of contents for our book," he said.

I rose to my feet. "Oh, Thor!" It was rather like producing a child. Something there where nothing enduring had been there before. Our prospective book was now a full-fledged embryo.

There was a moment of silent wonder between us as together we stared at the single typewritten page. Actually it was little changed since our last conference. But typed and pristine, it had acquired resoluteness. One could not scan the chapter headings without the conviction that they flowed from incontestable insight. (We would change them a dozen times.)

"It looks great."

We considered what remained to be done and the division of labor between us. Little actual writing on the book would be done in the field. Our precious time would continue to be devoted to the gathering of data.

We had come to understand the dynamics of life behind the village's storybook facade. Our study of Taarnby was documenting the consequences of technological change that began at the end of the nineteenth century and of the villagers own acceptance of its potential to influence their lives. Now we had a framework within which to trace *Taarnby past*, a maritime community in spirit, economy, and social organization; and *Taarnby present*, its cultural base moving inexorably toward urban incorporation.

Increasingly, village youth aspired to success at a desk rather than at a wheelhouse or an eel trap. At the same time, the new wider bridges from Copenhagen were inviting the emigration of city dwellers to the picturesque island. Only the sea-nurtured spirit of the community struggled against the island's clear— and more prosperous—destiny.

As we reviewed our field progress, Thor ventured: "I thought I might get the rest of the archival work out of the way." With an ease unmatched by the villagers themselves he read the old penned Danish scripts, analyzing diaries and letters which would have to remain with village families. Thor thrived in searching in libraries, the files of the city hall, and the records of mariners and seamen, often located—as they had been for decades— within Taarnby's inns and meeting halls.

I had come to enjoy most the person-to-person exchange of fieldwork. What interviewing remained of the mayor, ships' officers, and fishermen would fall largely to Thor. In these encounters the male-to-male advantage prevailed. There remained to me, however, a huge inventory of uninterviewed villagers.

On this night, the house seemed unusually cozy. Thor and I had our second aquavit, after which our planning efforts seemed to simplify themselves with surprising speed.

"We need full-time domestic help if you're going to do all this," Thor said.

"Fru Odstadt might be willing," I volunteered. "Except for Tuesdays, when she visits her mother. She'll be unhappy if she thinks we expect all her time."

"Hey! That would be great. She did the cooking while you were in the hospital," Thor remembered, beaming with the silent recollection of what must have been the most orderly ten days he'd experienced in Taarnby.

"With a lot of discretion I'm sure I can formalize the arrangement," I said. The little extra money would be welcome in her household. True domestic help was unknown in the village.

"Oh boy!" Thor said.

We got to work on the interview selection. After a while Thor stood up and gave a contented stretch. "Do you know it's after eleven," he observed.

While we had previously worked rather opportunistically in scheduling interviews, we now had an hour-by-hour, day-by-day agenda for the coming month. The finished product exuded ingenuity, as well as promise. The timing of my interviews continued to be determined in part by my nursing schedule with Sarah.

We typed up the first week's appointments and thumbtacked them above the desk. They did look lovely. A couple of omissions occurred to me, like time for shopping and time for bathhouse visits, but these seemed somehow inconsequential in the light of all the productivity that lay germinating on that tidy sheet of paper.

Why, even the weather seemed to be cooperating. "It's warming up," Thor observed, sipping his third aquavit. He pulled off his turtleneck sweater.

"I was about to mention that very thing," I assured him.

I went out to the kitchen and put together Katie's school lunch for the next day. By the time I came back into the living room, Thor had finished his drink. He was in splendid humor, glowing warmly in anticipation of the ordered days ahead.

Why, he asked rhetorically, had we been so obtuse as not to have struck on this obvious approach to fieldwork earlier? My enthusiasm was getting to be tempered by engulfing fatigue. Sarah, I hoped, might just sleep through the night. Please God.

It was almost midnight as we headed for the kitchen ladder, and at long last for sleep in the bedroom above. I was five rungs up the ladder when I felt Thor's insistent tug on my ankle. (Thor routinely climbed immediately below me "so as to break the fall," which, he was confident, my acrophobic tendencies sooner or later would trigger.)

I stopped, my right arm wrapped securely around a chest-high rung.

"There's just one thing more," he whispered hoarsely, the sound rising and amplified to foghorn intensity by the thick cemented walls.

We'll wake Sarah! I thought. But no sound came from above. I backed down the ladder and pushed Thor into the living room. His eyes glowed as with some crowning insight.

"I think we should have a battle cry!"

"What?"

"A battle cry. You know, like 'Excelsior' or 'Eureka.' But those aren't good. If things should bog down, well, we can kind of remind ourselves."

I resisted speech. He was entirely serious.

"Well?" he said expectantly, eyes fixed on me.

"We need to think about it," I said carefully.

"Nothing comes to mind?"

"Well, nothing good, you know." I edged him toward the kitchen. "I say let's sleep on it. Let it perk."

"Good thinking!" he agreed. "You will think about it, though?"

"Trust me," I said, in the kitchen again. I began to climb.

"You know Latin," came from below.

"I used to," I corrected, very softly.

When I was halfway up the ladder, my ankle was again immobilized by Thor's encircling hand. The prospect of a plunge to the kitchen floor was becoming more plausible by the moment. His rasping whisper rose vibrantly.

"'Omnia Gallia,' begins something, doesn't it?"

"Caesar's Gallic Wars," I said.

His grip tightened spasmodically. The war imagery had energized him.

"'All Gaul is divided into three parts,'" I quoted.

"That's it?"

"That's it."

I felt his hand go limp and scampered up the remaining rungs. I undressed, piled the layers of garments on a chair, and pulled a flannel gown over my longjohns. I crawled into my Mother Bear bed, set in the wall. Thor was sitting on his, the largest bed, staring at his boots. Beyond, where the roof dipped and a small window framed a gable of roof thatching, Katie slept in the alcove which shaped the smallest bed. Sarah lay noiselessly in a woven-cane crib, and I peeked at her before climbing into bed.

The icy pillowcase felt almost welcome against my face; my exhausted body sank into the mattress, and I waited for the down coverlet to position its bulk around me. The luminous hands of the small bedroom clock showed midnight. Where had the time gone?

"*Tempus fugit*," I sighed aloud.

Thor roared out of his bed alcove like an aroused bear from a cave.

"That's it! That's it!" he yelled joyously. "That's our motto," lifting me from my pillow by the shoulders. " 'Time flies!' I knew you'd do it. 'Time flies!' That'll keep us going!"

It kept us going until 1:00 A.M., by which time Sarah had been quieted, changed, nursed, and coaxed into halfhearted sleep. And Katie had been sent back to bed, reassured to hear that Daddy had had a funny and vivid dream. Thor and I eventually logged almost six hours of sleep.

In the morning I was grateful that I had made Katie's lunch the night before, so that, while she ladled down her oatmeal, I could hug my warm coffee cup until the moment came to send her off into the purple-black morning. At 8:00 A.M. day was barely distinguishable from midnight. The sky was stark, spiked with pockets of stars, and edged with a faint circular band of pale blue light. This was the only concession to morning.

Katie pushed off happily on her purple scooter, schoolbooks in her backpack, her metal lunch pail looped over the handlebars. Every morning it was like pushing a little bird from the nest. But Katie thrived on it.

The cold from the open door shot through my body like instant starch. I was wondering if day one of the "Schedule," as it came to be called, didn't warrant twenty-four hours of postponement. Thor stoked the *kakkelovn*, which, having been unusually nourished with coke through the night, maintained a marvelous level of warmth. It was a day for staying in. But Thor was busy now, pulling out notebooks, poring over folders of information.

"Well, I'm off for my appointment with the Seal," he said.

"The Seal" was secretary of the Taarnby Fishermen's Association, a man of considerable bulk, who, with his spiky mustache and shiny, rubberized greatcoat — which tapered in abruptly at the ankles — resembled nothing so much as that marvelous aquatic creature, particularly since he waddled when he walked and was given to lunging his head about as though sniffing the harbor air. He quite welcomed Thor's company, especially now that most harbor activities were curtailed. Through his logbooks, minutes of meetings (including those long past), and a prodigious knowledge of the local seas, the Seal commanded valuable data and could reconstruct Taarnby's glorious prominence as one of Denmark's most active fishing and maritime communities.

I was scheduled to visit the Ibransen sisters, who ran the local grocery. It would be a "cold call." I had no appointment and was not expected. What had seemed adventurous in the context of the previous night's enthusiasms now took on more subdued dimensions, as I imagined myself effecting the slightest control over "The Dervishes," as we had come to refer to Ingrid and Estrid Ibransen.

"Are you going to be okay?" Thor asked.

He was torn. That was plain. He wanted me back in bed, getting the sleep I'd missed. But — he couldn't help himself — he wanted more to have me out in the village, piling up marvelous masses of data. On course, the two of us.

"Should I tell Fru Odstadt to come over?"

"About a quarter of ten," I told him. "I need some time with Sarah first."

"Say, great!" he said, pleased and relieved. Ten o'clock was the time listed on our schedule for the Ibransen sisters' interview.

I smiled. Hard to argue with day one of the Schedule, to which a certain amount of sanctity clearly attached.

8

A Key Informant
The Store by the Sea

There is a dimension of fieldwork that for me never changes. Wherever I've worked, in ethnic neighborhoods of Texas or in a tobacco-growing village in India with my Hindi-speaking translator in tow, one reaction is the same. I find myself on some doorstep where I have no particular right to be, dependent on the goodwill of whatever face will appear, and I suddenly wonder, what the hell am I doing here, what machination of fate has brought me to such an improbable place with the presumption that anyone should speak with me? Something in me goes starkly cold, as though I'd been thrust upon a stage and had forgotten my lines. But it passes almost as quickly as it comes. Words are said. Things move along, usually well enough that I am not driven off.

Now, in front of the Ibransens', I faltered, moving to stand in front of the dry-goods store next door, staring at the simple display of embroidery hoops, colored floss, and stamped pillowcases. When it came right down to it, I didn't know what I'd do once inside the Ibransens'. I was supposed to get one of the sisters off alone. But that would not be easy. They moved about like one another's shadows. And where could we go for privacy in any case? The store was minuscule. But the time was right. After eleven o'clock the place would fill with prelunch shoppers. On my arm I had my shopping basket and in my purse my shopping list.

I walked into the shop.

69

The Ibransen grocery had the ambiance of a bookstore, except that it could not have been more than sixteen feet square. I had seen it many times, and the first impression was always the same, a frozen-in-time quality, a sense of Dickensian entrenchment. One waited to see Bob Cratchit scamper out and settle himself on a tall stool.

The room was all grays and browns, as were the Ibransen sisters in their undistinguished sweaters and skirts. A light bulb in its amber celluloid collar hung from a thick cord, barely clearing the heads of the sisters, who were small women. I had seen them in action many times, collaring the light with their fingers to focus it like a flashlight on a requested item. The gesture was for the benefit of customers, since Ingrid or Estrid Ibransen, I was confident, could have taken an inventory of the shop in total darkness — a condition the shop approached on that midwinter morning.

Every niche of the place was filled with canned and boxed goods and with hemp sacks whose tops were neatly rolled back to display their contents. The sisters customarily stood surrounded by a counter of varnished dark wood, two sides of which housed display cases containing, side-by-side, tilted glass canisters filled with everything from pickled herring to dried apricots, and a kind of hardtack to which even the village children were addicted and with which one could confidently have driven a nail through a half-inch plank. "It's my very favorite," insisted Katie, whose two front baby teeth eventually failed to endure against it.

Precious things like coffee, tinned cocoa, and a limited collection of pâtés in flat golden cans made up a separate section.

It was not until one stood at the counter, beside the narrow, cluttered cash register — which made a great clanging sound with every number pushed — that one saw what Thor and I called the black hole. For throughout the day, the sisters moved like agile aerialists on the brink of a trapdoor which led to the store's basement with its cache of reserve stock, and where beer and soft drinks were routinely kept. In winter a scaffolding of lumber and gunnysack protected the bottles from the frozen basement floor; in summer the cellar functioned as a giant cooler, and eggs and cheese wheels were also stored there. The Ibransens made a home-brew root beer, and on the warmest days, in July and

August, defective caps would explode like firecrackers, livening activity in the shop and adding to the speculation that the sisters were not beyond accommodating a home still, obviously imperfect.

The sisters were a marvel to behold in full action, when the store bulged with shoppers singing out their needs, usually from a written list. Thor and I called the sisters "The Dervishes" because of the twirling grace with which they spun around one another, their arms busy in an economy of movement that got the job done with amazing speed. Never colliding, swift and sure. Nor was there ever a backward glance as they careened about the open trapdoor.

Periodically a customer would call out for drinks. "Two orange soda waters and three beers, please, Miss Ibransen!" And one or the other would seem to flow down the stairs as though sucked from sight by some hidden whirlpool, only to surface again spectacularly, bottles in both hands, as if that same magnetic force now pulled her from the depths.

They rarely smiled, but conveyed an air of unperturbable serenity. I was mildly afraid of them.

On this day, when Estrid Ibransen moved from the shadows into the arc of light, I leaped. "Good morning, Fru Anderson," she called.

"Good morning."

She was alone. Either that, or her sister still lurked somewhere in the dark fringe. We went through my modest shopping list as I struggled for some observation that might invite conversation and the eventual explanation of my real mission.

Surprisingly, that observation came from Estrid, as I was paying my tab, dawdling as I worked out the exact combination of coins. She was looking at my feet.

"You don't wear proper boots, you know," she said. And after a pause, "Neither does Katie."

"Ah!" I said. Over the months nothing had served to diminish the village women's conviction that my daughters' survival depended on their continued surveillance.

"A proper boot breathes," Estrid said, drawing out the word with delicate hand gestures as though she were opening a concertina. She stared regretfully at my boots. Then she shook her head. "Do your feet sometimes feel damp and cold even

though you know they're not wet? Do you feel the cold of the
streets through two pairs of wool socks? Are the toes icy to the
touch when the boot is removed?"

It was the exhortation of a full-blown commercial. But I knew
the store did not stock boots. Her eyes riveted on mine.

"Katie," she began, and I at once anticipated the finish, "needs
new boots!" I said the words aloud with her, my voice trailing
slightly behind. She laughed, her eyes and mouth lifting in the
triangular face. The transformation was amazing. She was
instantly a pixie. I sat down on a substantial-looking crate, and
she moved beside me.

"But it is true, Madame," she said. "Winter is harsh in Taarnby.
Harsher than you perhaps realize. And it will get worse, you
know, before spring comes, for we have always the sea around us.

I realized, looking at her, that she was much younger than I
had imagined. No more than thirty-five, I guessed.

Last winter, she told me, the salt waters of the Øresund had
frozen to such a depth that the lighthouse keeper was isolated,
and fuel and provisions had to be hauled out a half-kilometer
on sleds.

"We do not hope for another such winter," she said. I
apparently looked quite stricken. "But you are here for all of it,
is that not so?"

We would remain until summer, I told her.

"I perhaps do not exactly understand what it is actually that
keeps you here," she said. It was an expression of genuine
interest.

I could hear the scraping sound which meant that someone's
stalwart, breathing boots were being cleaned of mud and snow
before entering the shop. Estrid heard it too and stood, and so
did I. But I wasn't going to let the momentum dissipate itself
and let her leave me before I had a real appointment. "I would
love to tell you about the things that Thor and I do," I said. "And
perhaps there are things you could tell me about Taarnby and
life here."

She agreed that I might come and talk with her two afternoons
a week at 2:30, when Ingrid regularly took over the shop. I agreed
to take no more than an hour of her time, an announcement
which did not appear to distress her.

I left, passing Fru Møller-Pedersen with her daughter Anna (the "Sherman tank") in tow. The success of this, my first encounter under the new Schedule, exhilarated me, and I walked confidently through the snow—nonbreathing boots notwithstanding.

I had four meetings with Estrid Ibransen in the flat she shared with her older sister and their eighty-year-old father above the store. Each had a kind of sitting room/bedroom that allowed privacy. Estrid let me know at once that she didn't like questionnaires, so I put away the one I'd brought to our first session. She was faithful to our appointments but relaxed only if we talked without my taking or recording notes. Before setting out for the store, I would go over a checklist of things I wanted to bring up with her, and when a session ended, I would race back to type it all up, almost in a stream of consciousness, with as many verbatim recalls as I could retain. Ambiguities and holes in the continuity I could clarify at the beginning of our next meeting.

Initially she chafed at overtures about her personal life, deflecting replies to a discussion of her father's and the store's past. She had questions to ask about Thor and me. After a while I worried that nothing substantial would come of the time I spent with her. As her comfort grew in the confidentiality of our relationship, however, she spoke more and more freely of herself.

Estrid's childhood had been like that of many of Taarnby's residents. Daughter of the second officer of a maritime ship, she had grown up with the loving, if intermittent, presence of her father. Her mother was the hub of a family life that she remembered as structured around his anticipated returns or imminent departures. Twenty years younger than he, her mother adored him, and life was fullest and richest for everyone when her father was in port. Winter was cherished because he was less often at sea. When she was twelve and Ingrid was fourteen, her mother died in a flu epidemic, and her father's older unmarried sister came to live with them. Although she was a kind and capable woman, her aunt could not fill the void for any of them. Two years later, her father sustained a permanent injury to his left arm in a shipboard accident when the cargo shifted in heavy seas, so he had to leave his job. Pension funds enabled him to enlarge the inventory in the small shop his sister ran on a part-time basis, selling jams and homemade cookies. Their clientele gradually and profitably grew to its present scope. Estrid developed the resolve "never to marry a sailor and find myself living my mother's waiting life."

One afternoon when we were talking about the growing range of occupations currently represented in Taarnby, she volunteered, "I married a surveyor." My face must have registered my surprise.

"You didn't know I was married," she smiled. She went to a dresser, opened a drawer, and came back with a snapshot of a good-looking, tousled-haired blond man. He stood, arms crossed on his chest, leaning against a car, smiling broadly into the camera. "He came out with a crew from Copenhagen when the summer villas began to get fancier and some city people wanted proper homes they could retire to."

My eyes had gone involuntarily to the room around us. It was a woman's room. She read my thoughts. "We never lived here. We moved to Copenhagen. He had a flat there. I think that was part of it. I loved the city. Loved it! Loved being there. But . . ." But there were problems. After eighteen months the marriage fell apart.

"I'd known him only a month. Nobody's fault. Foolish from the start. We were each of us glad to see the end of it."

Her father's health had been declining, so that he could do less and less work in the store, and her sister reached the limits of her ability to deal with him and the store, the source of their support. After the divorce, Estrid returned to Taarnby.

"I'm glad I did. It was the thing to do. I'd never have forgiven myself if I hadn't." She shrugged her shoulders. "Besides it wasn't unselfish. I needed to support myself, didn't I?"

We talked about the resumption of her life in Taarnby, her daily routine, the web of contacts. "We've worked it out, Ingrid and I. My father thought it spendthrift, but we've hired Egon, who does the books at the hotel, to do ours, pay bills, and keep track of inventory. This year, when the summer visitors start to come, we'll put on one of the high school girls four hours a day. In good weather it'll give Ingrid or me a chance to take a trip or two. One of us in the store, one away."

Estrid's months in Copenhagen had established an appetite for more adventure, for experiences beyond those available within Taarnby, for a different life style.

"Of course, in a way I was glad to return to the island," she insisted. "You know, when you've been thirty years breathing in the sea, living away from it takes some getting used to."

But for Estrid, and increasingly for the island's young people, a tantalizing and workable resolution is possible: a home in Taarnby, a career and adventure outside it. Educations have been geared to the skills that pay off in urban employment. For Taarnby's young men, pinnacles of career success are less often identified with life at sea, nor do the women they date today see themselves as sweethearts or wives of men who choose that life.

Still, for villagers, despite compromises in life styles, the sea remains imbued with a mythic intimacy born of past glories that lifts the people of Taarnby a rank above those whom the sea chose not to so distinguish.

9

Maintaining Goodwill

The Ballad of Ole

A dimension of first fieldwork about which the new anthropologist is rarely if ever warned is the ongoing state of marginal control in which the fieldworker regularly finds herself vis-a-vis informants. In the early months of fieldwork, goodwill is tenuous at best. But after six months of residence, and with at least the children entrenched as villagers, we enjoyed considerable freedom of movement in Taarnby. Yet with few exceptions, our activities as anthropologists remained little understood. The robust, hardworking mariners and their wives had difficulty comprehending how any urgency could attach to what we did. And though we had forged some friendships and some measure of respect, most villagers struggled to find very much scientific in the apparently purposeless ways we spent our days.

That we were interested in history and valued the community's glorious association with the sea: these concerns of ours most validated their expenditure of time with us. But they sometimes trivialized appointments or turned out not to be available for interviews at all. I think, too, that with their lingering uncertainties about us they—like villagers the world over—yielded to the rationalization of other priorities in order to escape us.

Even when doors were opened to us, the way was not free of peril in terms of the maintenance of goodwill. I experienced recurrent nightmares that some banal encounter might go suddenly awry and spawn enough animosity to make it impossible for us to complete our work, or—as our professors had emphasized could indeed occur—we would find ourselves thrown out of the community.

Two weeks into the Schedule I had a frustrating Wednesday morning. Two of the three people I had planned to see were out (or I was told they were out), and I wasted half the afternoon with the third person, Fru Schidt, coping with a pitiless onslaught of cream-filled pastry and ollalaberry punch, cut off from escape by a phalanx of twelve women singers: the Wednesday Afternoon Sip and Sing Club (or the alliterative Danish equivalent), who were pleased I had come on one of the rare afternoons when their meeting was open to prospective members.

As the meeting wore on I knew, despite the attraction of so large a pool of potential informants, that more such Wednesday afternoons would prove hazardous to my health. Between servings of pastry, with whose ordered consumption I failed to keep pace, the women sang five hymns and four sea chanteys, none of whose many verses I followed very well. In the plaintive chanteys, a good deal of "slipping beneath the waves" was prominent.

I was mentally rehearsing my withdrawal speech, with its mandatory civilities, when the singers regrouped in a kind of huddle from which a head emerged from time to time as if to appraise me. A consensus reached, the group surrounded me, obviously in high good humor—a condition they maintained when eating, if not when singing. I was introduced to Fru Olafsen, the choir director—who when her name was mentioned placed a hand on her bosom and nodded vigorously at me.

"My husband," Fru Olafsen began, "is a ham radio operator." This explication involved some group pantomime. "One of his Norwegian friends, a fellow seaman, has the same hobby. Also, he is a fine musician—amateur, of course. Well . . ."

To have something to do in the winter months, the men began collecting from international music broadcasts rousing chanteys and dark ballads of shipwreck and death at sea. The Norwegian wrote down the music. Fru Olafsen's husband, a man of apparent language skills, was charged with translating them. The origins of one of these songs, an American one, lay shrouded in mystery. "We would like to sing it for you," Fru Olafsen concluded.

"For me?" Dismay swept over me like damp seaweed. "Well that would be lovely, of course, but I, I can't imagine that I would know very much about sea ballads, even American ones."

"But that's just it!" Fru Olafsen pursued, surrounded by a supporting nucleus of nodding heads. "My husband thinks that the "Ballad of Ole" — that's its name — may be Scandinavian. Perhaps actually Danish. That it was somehow lost to us and survived in American translation." Everyone radiated clear and abundant pride in this apparent musical breakthrough, to the extent that they were planning to incorporate the song in their Winter Concert at Seamen's Hall. "If you might just verify the words."

My protestations that the title of the song was totally unfamiliar to me dissuaded no one. And Fru Schidt, the hostess and pianist, took her place at the piano. "It is," she said, "a very sad song."

I sat back in my chair, positioned so that I viewed the assembled group like some impresario on whose judgment hinged the fate of a musical discovery. Several bars of piano improvisation set the tone for the obviously dark nature of what was to come. And then twelve voices rose in "The Ballad of Ole."

> I know a dark secluded place,
> A place where no one knows my face,

Later, discussing it with Thor, I remembered how grateful I was that I was without the usual cup of coffee in my hands. For as the nature of what was unfolding became more and more apparent, I could feel the spasmodic grip of my fingers on the pencil and paper which they had placed in my hands — should I wish to make notes. There were perhaps forty seconds during which the overslow tempo, the alien pronunciation, and above all, their fanciful reworking of the lyrics, masked identification of the song. But well before the chorus gave forth with their first "Ole!" they had my full attention.

> The dashing waves, a fearsome spray,
> It's called Inferno's Castaway, Ole!

The origins of "The Ballad of Ole" were unmistakable. Herr Olafsen had rendered a nautical dirge out of one of *Pajama Game*'s most tuneful hits. I had seen the musical, and now visions of the stage set with its comically dark Mexican cafe, punctuated with tiny tables and burning candles, with a tipsy singer belting out "Hernando's Hideaway," floated across the faces of the Wednesday Afternoon Sip and Sing Club like an improbable double exposure. In front of me twelve bosoms heaved in unison:

> Where all you see are silhouettes,
> And all that's near is cold and wet,

Ole's dark fate was predictable. The doleful repetition of poor Ole's name marked the end of each verse. The final "Ole" was pianissimo:

> One of Inferno's castaways, O-l-e-e-e-e!

held throughout the pianist's effective arpeggio.

There was an overlong hush as all eyes fixed on me. Fru Olafsen, as wife of the lyric translator, was the first to speak, preempting interjections by other members of the group, all of whom remained in position. Fru Olafsen, it suddenly occurred to me, had a great deal riding on this, her husband's imminent, and very public, debut. "So then?" she asked, in the Danish formula that exacts a reply.

"It was," I said, "a very moving song." The actual Danish adjective covers a multitude of feelings associated with rare and uplifting experiences.

"You know the song then?"

I was on dangerous ground. "The melody is very familiar," I conceded.

She turned and let her eyes sweep assertively across the group.

"I'm afraid I can't be more specific than that, Fru Olafsen," I added, "though I can tell you most certainly that I have heard that song before."

"And the words?"

"Words and music, I can assure you, were exceptional."

"Exceptional!" she repeated. She pressed her palms together emitting little sounds of relief and pleasure. "Oh my!" Even to consider adulterating that joy, the ever-rising level of which I was now effecting, was suddenly quite unthinkable.

There was, I later confessed to Thor, a moment or two of inner struggle. But then the way out became clear, and peace descended upon me with solacing calm: avoid an outright falsehood but volunteer no troublesome revelations. When I spoke it was with the assurance of a physician dismissing a troubled patient. "Believe me," I said. "I wouldn't touch a word of it. Not one word."

And just to make sure that I had not absolved myself from public responsibility, I accepted their invitation to sing the song with them at the Winter Concert.

"You realize, of course," Thor said afterwards, "that you have personally granted a copyright for a Broadway hit to a group of fishermen's wives."

"Fru Schidt's husband is a second officer, not a fisherman," I corrected.

But Thor was less than happy with me. "Did you at all consider telling them that Fru Olafsen's husband spent the winter converting a hot tango to dirge tempo?"

"Only briefly," I said.

Thor was there for the concert, together with Katie, who predictably would settle for nothing but a front-row. "That's my mother," Katie said in a voice that carried. Thor put his finger to his lips.

We stood on stage. Fru Schidt's fingers picked out the now familiar prelude. I had had little trouble committing Herr Olafsen's words to memory. I saw him now move from his place in the auditorium to the edge of the stage to confirm that the borrowed tape recorder which he had placed there for this, the first public rendering of "his song," was indeed functioning.

> He walked the dark and slippery place,
> Those planks where no one's ever safe!

Some of the women had fine voices. When the first "Ole" came it was with resonant precision.

And then I heard Katie's voice again, coming as it did in the break between stanzas, as the pianist's hands arched over the carefully spaced chords. "Daddy, I know that song!"

I saw Thor leap as though a live wire had been touched to the metal chair in which he sat. He bent and spoke into Katie's ear, after which she straightened sedately in her chair, hands folded on her lap.

"The Ballad of Ole" was a resounding success. At the reception which followed, Herr Olafsen was acclaimed for his scholarship and ingenuity in adding the song to the local repertoire. I felt very good about it. Whatever my sins, my conscience was treating them lightly.

"I was glad for him too," Thor said as the three of us walked home, bundled to the teeth. "And for Fru Olafsen, who really enjoyed her hour in the limelight."

He looked at Katie. "And what got into you tonight? I thought we were going to get thrown out."

Katie was embarrassed. And a little angry with herself. She was developing a thoroughly Danish sense of decorum and didn't like being found wanting in the basic graces. "I don't see why I couldn't tell people that I heard the song before," she said.

Thor's eyes met mine.

"You know the words?"

"Sure."

"All of them?"

"Sure I do, Daddy."

I laughed.

"Let her rip," I said. "We'll sing it together." And I threw back my head and started to sing.

> I know a dark secluded place,
> A place where no one knows your face,
> A glass of wine, a fast embrace,
> It's called Hernando's Hideaway! Ole!

It was suddenly a marvelous release to have the tension-laden evening behind me, to be kicking through the snow in a Danish village, almost in the middle of the North Sea, and give "Hernando's Hideaway" back its happy tango tempo and its own silly words.

Katie was tugging at me and I stopped.

"Hey! Did you forget already? You got the words all mixed up. And . . ."

She positioned herself under a lamppost in front of us, bringing Thor and me to a purposeful halt.

"It goes a whole lot slower. Now listen."

She sang with a measured pacing of each word, eyes wide with the burden of bringing gusto to the dirgelike rhythm:

> He walked the dank and slippery place,
> On planks where no one's ever safe!

Her head and shoulders swayed back and forth to the laborious beat of "The Ballad of Ole." And each explosion of the word "Ole!" brought a kick of her heel in the snow and her hands to her eyes to peer into an unseen ocean's depth.

She sang it through, never faltering, her small voice made oddly lyrical in the night air. The words lifted clean and insistent across the harbor, where the masts of two sailing craft rose darkly in the moonlight.

"Well?" she said, when she finished. "Do you get it now?"

Beside me Thor blew noisily into his handkerchief.

"Yes, I get it," I said. "Slower. Right?"

"Right. I learned it from Kristen Olafsen. Her daddy wrote it. We didn't know it was a secret."

At the door she said:

"Is it all right if I teach it to Franz? I mean, it's all right now, isn't it?"

"Spread the word, baby," I said.

Thor lifted her and gave her a snowy squeeze.

10

Acculturation
The Enduring Cold

O ften during the year we wished we had brought some anthropology journals with us and more books. But paper is heavy, and a half-dozen volumes weigh like marble bookends. Then there's the chore and expense of shipping everything back. We spent some of our evening hours discussing joint recollections of culture change literature. When we could, we ransacked the shelves at the University of Copenhagen, to whose libraries we had acquired cards. Books in English abounded, but some relevant ones existed only in Danish translation, and for me it was tedious going. Retrospectively, it was probably better that we were without a bountiful library around the house. It might have proved too tempting a refuge from the demands of fieldwork.

However, by the end of March we were more at peace with ourselves than we had been since the beginning of fieldwork. The Schedule was working, although it was no longer sacrosanct.

We now made it a practice to overbook on appointments to insure we'd stay busy and to make every hour work for us. If we were running late, we would send a message on ahead by one of the village children. The villagers took it all in stride, good-naturedly.

Our activities as anthropologists, though perhaps little better understood, were acquiring commendable overtones. We were, in the villagers' eyes, unusual guests — strange would have been the word from the less charitable — but in the last analysis, harmless and all too often helpless. This guarded appraisal did not apply to the children, who had become one of them, Katie by osmosis and Sarah by adoption. All of Taarnby lived with the fiction that the children were now somehow a fixed and permanent part of village life. At the end of the day, Katie needed minutes of unwinding before she could abandon Danish for English.

Thor had put together a kind of file drawer from some shoe boxes and a grocery crate which snugly accommodated three boxes across and two deep as though it had been made for them. Nightly our field data were transcribed onto five-by-eight-inch cards, and we were putting in whatever hours it took to keep them current. We made three copies of everything; we filed one topically and one by informant and periodically shipped a collection of third copies home for safekeeping.

"It's beautiful, isn't it?" Thor said earnestly, admiring the burgeoning transcripts much as a botanist might admire the proliferation of rare plants in his greenhouse.

Each time he added a card, he would align it with studious care and, oblivious of his transparent pride, give an affectionate pat to the box. For both of us now the complex demands of home and work at last had reached a kind of equilibrium which, although it did not eliminate stress, made its presence more tolerable.

Sarah had begun more routinely to get through the night without serious demands for attention. She could take a bottle from Fru Odstadt if I were delayed for a nursing, and Thor was fast with a diaper. We had long before worked out a division of labor in the kitchen, whereby my evening responsibility ended with the cooking. When the two gas burners were cleared of skillets or pots, water was put on to boil so that by the end of dinner the kitchen was ready for Thor's carefully programmed cleanup. We were buoyed in our consensus that however bumpy the course of our work, we were fully functioning field anthropologists at last.

Over the enduring cold we had minimal to zero control, and its effects on basic creature comforts were growing.

We had never before experienced so prolonged an intensity of snow and ice. In Taarnby the fact of winter, the long, long winter, shaped every waking and sleeping moment—particularly given our primitive housing.

Most of the village families now had indoor plumbing, though this generally involved using a bucket of water as a flushing technique, after which the bucket was refilled and placed beside the toilet, to be poured into the bowl and replaced again by the next visitor. A few of the more prosperous had installed automatic flushing mechanisms of a kind distinguished by two overhead chains, one of which provided the "little flush," and was so marked, and the other, the "big flush," when that was called for. It too was identified. The sounds emitted by each were readily distinguishable from afar, with the big flush usually audible within a wide radius, issuing an explosive sound out of proportion to its effectiveness. A double big flush (two successive pullings), however, created wide interest, could bring a whole family on the run, and was to be avoided when one was a guest.

We had only an outhouse, complete with a wooden seat which was actually no more than a hole in a plank positioned over an elevated five-gallon container (picked up weekly by the *tømmer* man, *tømmer* from the word for emptying). The ancient seat had been installed at a slightly tilted angle, a practice purposefully designed to discourage dawdlers — certainly a superfluous precaution in the dead of winter.

Journeys to the outhouse had become a kind of agonizing high adventure. Adventure in the Websterian sense, "to engage in daring undertakings," or "to take risks." Agonizing in that one waited until the last minute before making the dreadful dash, and because of the excruciating cold that accompanied getting to the outhouse, and most especially the moments spent within it.

The route from the heavy front Dutch door to the weathered and derelict structure took one over twenty feet of terrain as changeable as an ice floe — which in fact it sometimes resembled. More often, particularly in the early morning exodus, one faced the prospect of knee-high drifts crusted over by the night's ebbing deposit of a fine sheet of steely ice. Even Katie, the intrepid, who moved through the village with the easy panache of a polar bear crossing the ice, was undone by the need to leave the warmth of her down comforter and, in the lightless morning, undertake the outhouse odyssey.

Katie had eschewed use of the chamber pot.

She took a look at the ample pot, fashioned of dully glazed white pottery with a handle large enough for a seaman's grasp and through which one could have passed a plate. "No way!" she had said, her usual and unequivocal substitute for "No."

We all gave it careful scrutiny. Even empty, the chamber pot presented a problem in the logistics of lifting without tilting. One felt one's hand straining to break at the wrist. The tendency was to clasp it with both hands to one's chest for support. "Nevertheless," Thor said with his customary logic, "the alternative is going to prove far less attractive."

He assured Katie she could count on him to address the challenge of moving the pot from place to place, for the chamber pot came as standard accompaniment to the upstairs loft and enjoyed special housing in a bin designed for it and built into the wall between the beds. After use the chamber pot was transferred to a metal-lined drawer beneath the bin, complete with a sliding rack which accommodated the pot's cover— awaiting the judicious moment when it could be removed to the outhouse.

"Where are you supposed to use it?" Katie asked, countering logic with logic.

She had a point. The openness of the loft, a sharp contrast to the cozy alcoved beds, did create a public waiting room atmosphere, an atmosphere enhanced by the presence of a long wooden pew that must once have been in a church or bus station.

None of us was comfortable about using the chamber pot, even when alone upstairs or when an air of privacy was contrived by stretching a blanket between two chairs that had been hoisted up from the kitchen. Except under the most dire emergencies the existence of the chamber pot was ignored. Suppressed is perhaps more accurate. For in those vulnerable morning moments between sleep and wakefulness, the snug image of the little chamber pot rose unbidden into consciousness.

Katie feigned an air of casualness about the outhouse run. But her ambivalence was apparent. I would hear the long sleepy exhaling of breath which meant she was waking, and then the little grunts as her flanneled toes explored the cold beyond the pockets of warm body air held by the down comforter. Beside her bed on a stool lay her clothes, piled in what we called "outhouse order." These, not to be confused with eventual school clothes, were intended solely for the run, precise in their organization, and cunningly geared to the coming challenge — fast on, fast off (or rather *down*), warm, and waterproof.

Her eyes would open, stare at the clothes, then close again. They would reopen as she propped herself on an elbow and turned to look at the little bin that housed the chamber pot. "Maybe I'll . . ." Aloud. Her voice trailing tentatively.

But before Thor or I could inject a note of encouragement, she'd be on the edge of her bed, pulling on the thick gray socks, the padded jacket over her pajamas, the black rubber knee-high boots, the poncho, the knit cap with earflaps. Then, expertly, she went down the ladder. At the front door the steps stopped, long enough, I knew, for her to remove and don the right mitten from the right pocket, the left mitten from the left pocket.

Then came the long moments as Thor and I waited for the litany of sounds: the heavy front door (now opening, now closing, almost, but not quite, to the lock position), the clean sound of a small foot popping holes through the frail ice (one, two, three, four, five, six, seven, eight — My God! Where was she going! No, she was there), the squawk of the outhouse door, opening, closing (too slowly! Why was she letting in more cold air?). Then an incredible stretch of silence. (How absurd to hang on every sound.) Ah! the squeaking door again, reopening in agitated haste, banging shut and probably swinging free. (Oh Lord! The seat would freeze over for the rest of us.) Again the crunching, rapid now. (If she fell she'd freeze her face and hair.) The front door opening. The stomping of snow from her boots (which she hopefully remembered to leave in the small hallway so as not to track snow into the living room where it turned the rugs to wet felt). And then nothing, as she moved deftly in thick-stockinged feet across the house into the kitchen and back up the ladder.

I would feel my whole body unclench and a great sigh would come from Thor, who, I realized, had been half holding his breath so as to listen.

"I don't think I can take many more of Katie's 6:00 A.M. sorties," Thor told me one morning at the breakfast table after Katie had trudged off to school. "It's absurd. She should be made to use that pot!"

But in a moment he shrugged, pushed away his half-finished coffee, and put on the greatcoat of which he was so proud.

Men look smashing in winter, I thought. They look good in great, bulky things. Massive. Masculine. I was sick of my dowdy, makeshift wardrobe. I wished wantonly for a magnificent full-length lynx coat and then, conjuring the image, wished for a matching hat and a muff into which I would tuck my notebooks as I drifted across the snowy streets like a heroine from a Tolstoy novel.

It was a day when Thor and I had a joint appointment with "R.I.P." (Rest in Peace) and his wife. He was the pastor of the community's Lutheran church, a man whose enthusiasm for funerals had earned our nickname for him. I had never met his wife. "I understand she's big on custard-filled napoleons," Thor informed me.

Our appointment with them at three o'clock was a coffee hour, and anything less than the full cake-and-pastry board was improbable. "Oh God!" I said.

"Put it out of your mind," Thor said comfortingly. He was at the door.

I watched the wind buffet him toward the harbor. Johansen, one of the pilots, fell into step beside him. The villagers liked Thor. He had a busy day scheduled at the town hall, continuing his review of the records of birth, marriage, and death for the twenty families we had selected to study in historical depth. The total scenario would provide a lively and personalized record of the impact of fifty years of change on Taarnby.

By the time I had settled the home scene, allowed myself to be blown to Herr Wikman's, who was on his third installment of the life of a codless cod fisherman (unaccountably, the once plentiful fish had deserted the sound), followed the snow-clearing crew out to the home of a retired school principal, and made it back for Sarah's noon nursing, I was mumbling prayers of repentance for ever having had ignoble thoughts about my venerable, life-supporting, dyed-lamb coat.

My afternoon appointment sent word by his granddaughter that he could not see me. "My grandfather's arthritis is bad again and he has gone to bed. He asks if you would be so good as not to come today but to come tomorrow."

"Please tell Herr Hoyer that I hope he feels better and not to worry. I shall visit with him tomorrow only if it will not tire him," I said.

I poured a cup of heated apple juice into the granddaughter—standard stoking procedure. And she marched out again into the snow. It was good to stay in and get some of my heavy accumulation of notes transcribed.

At three o'clock, the snow started up again, and Fru Odstadt appeared to watch Sarah and stay until Thor and I returned. She made an especially fragrant pot of chocolate in anticipation of Katie's arrival, and I left the kitchen to her and headed for R.I.P.'s.

The fresh snow made for easier walking, but it was bitterly cold. With winter full upon us, the villagers were at home more often now. There was a good deal of baking, and every kitchen had a soup pot sitting on the back of a stove. It was a time for writing letters and mending, and it was rare to enter a living room without seeing a piece of unfinished sewing or knitting on a table or in an open basket.

The harbor now was thick with ice, and those craft not in drydock were locked in crystallized grandeur, their masts gleaming needles of ice; great tufts of blue-white snow crystals hung around the portholes of ships like Christmas wreaths. Almost every man had "winter things" to do. Equipment was repaired and nets were mended, and the men worked at these things in special huts on the harbor's edge, warmed by potbellied stoves. They drank coffee and sometimes hot grogs laced with a little whisky (which was too expensive to invite much overindulgence).

The general pulse of village life slowed but did not stop. Children still went to school; women shopped when some fragile rise in daytime temperatures was detected; and when the air was dry enough, clothes and blankets were still brought outdoors and hung briefly where the wind could whip through them so that they smelled of the sea.

I came home one day to find Sarah asleep in her buggy in our snowy yard, where she had been placed by Fru Odstadt, protected against the falling snow by a square of plastic. She was wrapped and dressed in wool, down to her pink cap and mittens. A tautly folded shawl held her snugly against the mattress. She lay eyes closed, too rosy, I hoped, to be lifeless.

"If she does not get the air now when she is small, how will she tolerate it when she must spend her days in it?" Fru Odstadt reasoned, when I questioned the deep-freeze approach to naptime.

Winter was also a time for long visits and intensified eating (an acceleration I would not have thought possible).

I did not look forward to the session at R.I.P.'s.

11

Mores and Symbols
Taarnby's Coffee Hours

I n later years and other field situations we came—almost routinely—to await the unfolding of the inevitable mini-horror that would encumber daily life in whatever culture we found ourselves. So predictable was the phenomenon that an air of apprehension attached to fieldwork until the exact nature of the yet-to-come challenge surfaced, at last, in all its irksome inescapability.

In Taarnby we found ourselves captives of coffee hours. These dominated socializing on the island. Fending off the ritualized consumption of sweets proved to be the number one field challenge in Taarnby. Through the confining winter we chafed at the merciless proliferation of coffee hours.

When I got to the pastor's home, Thor was already there. R.I.P. and his wife had an additional guest. It was in effect a party, a fact which obviated any hope to which we may have clung for a modest table. The guest was a gentleman from the isle of Fyn, slight of build and very thin. He had the barest fringe of bright red hair, and the fingers he extended limply to me for the obligatory handshake were yellow with nicotine.

"This is Herr Stenersen, who shares my interest in some of the lesser Ecclesiastes," Pastor Viborg stated in labored English.

R.I.P.'s long-cherished dream, I knew, was to be transferred from his post in Taarnby to a community more empathetic to his scholarly absorption with ancient texts. The route to this achievement, he was confident, lay in securing a fellowship abroad, and to this end he was bending considerable energy.

Upon hearing the pastor's half-dozen words of English, Herr Stenersen picked up the gauntlet, "More English we are speaking," he said to the assembled group, including the silent Fru Viborg.

I looked at Thor. "Pastor Viborg has invited us for an English evening," he said smiling broadly—as though an evening of exposure to yaws would not have been more pleasant.

Thor's announcement launched a complex pattern of verbal exchange, with Thor alone capable of uninhibited shifts from English to Danish and back to English again. Pastor Viborg who fancied himself a storyteller of some distinction, soon showed the strain, resorting either to a monosyllabic narrative style (my heart went out to him), or funneling everything—including the punch lines—through Thor for translation from Danish to English.

Herr Stenersen, who had promoted this travesty, sat sucking audibly on cigarettes which he smoked until the glowing tip had almost disappeared between his fingers, at which point he carefully removed a toothpick from his pocket, inserted it into the butt, and smoked on. He said not one word, but was given to vigorous nodding. I knew the technique. It was debatable whether he understood one word of English.

At last Fru Viborg rose to her feet. "So then, time it is for little coffee." Her first words. And R.I.P. and friend were on their feet headed for the dining room.

One glance at the table and Thor's eyes met mine with the quick appraisal of two battlewise soldiers who recognize a mine field when they see one. There they lay, in all their destructive potential, platter after platter of baked goods, densely distributed the length and width of a great oak table. At that moment, if we had been given the choice, permanent respite from the Danish winter or safe passage from the homes of Taarnby's pastry-crazed housewives, there would have been no contest.

The ground rules of a classic Danish coffee hour, such as the one we faced, are as tricky as chess and require just as much foresight. To begin with, the positioning of platters is not arbitrary (as I had initially assumed). The head of a table is designated by the placement of what is Danish is called *fylde mad*, literally "filling food"—actually thickly buttered, hand-sliced pieces of substantial white bread. Next and parallel to that platter is a larger one, holding "Viennese breads," a variety of prune-, apricot-, or raisin-filled Danish pastries, each as large as a man's hand. Next, a cake, normally of three layers, the standard filling and icing for which is jam and/or whipped cream.

The display now broadens to accommodate two columns of pastry along the table's center. In this case, on one side were Fru R.I.P.'s celebrated napoleons, multilayered rectangles of puff pastry, separated by custard and topped with marbled chocolate icing. Facing them lay an arrangement of bakery cream puffs generously powdered with sugar. These marked the halfway point, beyond which, on heirloom plates, were—sequentially—cupcakes, mixed cookies, and finely sliced Christmas fruitcake, followed by an arrangement that was half pastel bonbons and half chocolate-dipped cherries, and finally, nuts.

My very first exposure to a coffee hour had been unfortunate. It was our first month in the village and Thor and I were propelled off the street into the neat parlor of Fru Nordre to sit down to a small celebration of somebody's promotion. At that time I understood little of what was said, and less of what was going on. Thor had only the time to whisper, "Watch me and do what I do!"

These instructions proved useless, since immediately upon arriving at the table I was urged to begin, an honorific gesture not to be ignored. I did manage a brief glance across the table at Thor, who, directly opposite me, was lifting his left eyebrow, his head veering in the direction of our hostess at the head of the table, the implication of which was lost on me. The table was dazzling and laden with food and I had to make a choice. I took whatever was nearest to me, and that happened to be a cherry tart.

"It looks delicious," I said amiably as I placed the tart on my plate.

I raised my eyes just in time to see, hovering before me, a platter of bread and butter which my neighbor had apparently been in the act of extending. One glimpse at the tart, however, and she snatched the plate back, clutching it to her bosom, obviously perplexed, and then turned to her hostess with a silent appeal

for instructions. The hostess, also discomforted, indicated the
bread-and-butter should be returned to its natural resting place
in front of her. "Ha, hah!" Thor said.

I stared at my offending tart. Perhaps in Denmark cherry tarts
were not to be eaten by women. (I knew that whisky, for example,
unlike aquavit, was considered a rude drink for a lady.) Perhaps
I had taken the only cherry tart. I checked. Not so.

The plate of bread and butter again made its way
democratically down the table. I took it from my nervous neighbor
and turned, prepared to move the plate on. I was suddenly aware
of Thor, arched across the tabletop. "Have a piece of bread and
butter," he said to me, intercepting with one hand the forward
motion of the plate.

I reached for the slice of bread gravitating toward me from the
tilted plate in Thor's hand. After I had made room for it beside
the tart, I was aware of the active resumption of conversation as
though someone had readjusted the volume on a radio after a
crisis. After that I was fed rather like a child whose needs must
be anticipated lest she become disruptive and the adults can't
talk as they want. Thor remained on semialert, tracing my
progress between his conversational exchanges.

I ate more than I wanted and finally had had quite enough
and felt myself struggling with mounting indignation. My
behavior had proved in some way wanting and I was sorry for
that and ready enough to put things to right. But enough was
enough.

Thor had been smoking his pipe and sipping coffee for five
minutes, and I was still trying to hide unwanted sweets behind
the lacy remains of pastry cups. Then in a blessed rush of
memory, there came to mind a way out.

I would do what Thor had done. There would ripple off my
tongue in Danish an extravagant expression of praise for the food
I had eaten. Then I would fold my napkin and sit back, confident
in my hostess's delight. My sense of protocol, although tardy
and—for reasons I did not understand—flawed, would be
unchallengeable. I would end the afternoon on a high note.

Mentally I rehearsed my speech, a compliment that Thor had
taught me. I was confident I could faithfully repeat the
expression. The words spun effortlessly across my brain.

As if prearranged, there fell upon our group one of those pockets of silence that sometimes occurs when trivial conversations come to an uncanny and joint halt. I was ready. I smiled broadly, circling the table with my eyes in the approved Danish fashion to meet sequentially the gaze of each guest and bring them to rest finally on our hostess. I looked her evenly in the face.

"Det smagte fordømt godt!" I said with brave bold enunciation.

The effect was electrifying. Thor was unfortunate enough to ingest a few drops of coffee into his windpipe, sending him into paroxysms of coughing. The faces at the table all turned to me where their gazes held fixedly—like a frame of film frozen by the movie camera—their eyes wide and incredulous. There followed a stricken silence, interrupted only by Thor's coughing. Then, unexpectedly, a laugh, followed by other laughs, and I saw Herr Nordre, our host, head bent, slapping his knees, howling with glee.

"I didn't say it right," I ventured to Thor.

He had his voice back. "You said it *perfectly*. Loud and clear."

Around me the room was a shambles of hysterical villagers. Fru Nordre was dabbing ineffectually at her eyes, awash in laughter.

Thor picked up a spoon and tapped it on the cup at my place until things subsided enough for him to speak. The words came out in the stylized Danish overture which I could now recognize:

"I shall now tell you something."

There was still an occasional, involuntary rumble of laughter, but the group now hung on his every word. "It is a story," Thor said.

He told how, in the week after our arrival in Denmark, he had taken me to dinner in a Copenhagen restaurant, how I had struggled to use my limited Danish with the attentive waiter, and how—when we were having our coffee—I had pressured him to tell me something to say to express my delight over the fine meal.

I gave his sleeve a tug. "What did I say?"

Thor kept his eyes fixedly on the Danes. "So I coached her on a little sentence which," a small uncontrollable guffaw escaped his lips, "which she dutifully learned by heart. But when the time came she was just too shy to use it. That little thank-you speech, whose meaning my dear wife clearly does not fully understand, ladies and gentlemen, you have just heard. "Det smagte fordømt godt," he intoned, repeating (with gestures) the words I had indeed mastered. And laughter crashed around us again.

Finally, he leaned over me and with the same intonation slowly translated. "That tasted goddamned good!"

I was transfixed.

"Goddamned good!" Thor repeated, laughing wildly.

I could feel the hot blood soar up over my cheeks and forehead and come to full flush at my hairline. One look at me and Thor was instant contrition.

"Now honey," he said. "I suppose it was a mean trick. But you have to admit I didn't mean to set you up for . . ." He spread his hands, fighting another collapse, "this."

"Not for saying to a dozen people you'll be seeing on a daily basis for the next year," I said evenly.

For their part the assembled Danes had broken up into smaller groups and were already recounting the incident to one another. The women would soon have it into the network and out on the streets.

But they were kind. Before departing, men and women individually came up to assure me that, as one woman said, biting her lip for control, my "little contribution had just made for a delightful afternoon."

It was a week before I had been able to allow myself the reflection that ignorance of coffee hour protocol lay at the root of the wild scene at Fru Nordre's. I appealed to Tove, my former Canadian friend, for help in getting through these pastry orgies with less trauma.

"Well," she said, when I recounted the wide attention that was drawn to my selection of a cherry tart, "you skipped the *fylde mad*."

"Skipped what?"

"The bread and butter. Not to take bread and butter before you take anything else is as unthinkable as not to offer it. Bread and butter is a symbol of the nourishing hearth and a reminder of lean days of the past—and the transitory blessings of the present."

I had never heard Tove so eloquent.

"It's a matter of restraint," she said, lighting a small cigar. She blew a stream of smoke slowly into the air, studying it. "Of course it is a restraint that is then supposed to be undone by the lavishly tempting food offered by one's hostess."

"And then you can take the cherry tart," I offered.

"The proper course for any right-minded guest is down the table, from head to foot, ignoring nothing and pacing oneself. Otherwise a hostess wonders into the night why Grete ignored her rum cake, or if there is really waning enthusiasm for her cheese fingers."

Coffee hours, I learned from firsthand experience, could not be rushed. Conversation was as necessary to them as air to a fire. As a rough time gauge, a hostess counted the number of service plates and multiplied by fifteen minutes. Coffee hours rarely lasted less than two hours. Three was the average. And the imposing four-hour ones (evening) were densely attended during winter.

By the time of our evening with R.I.P. and his wife and their Ecclesiastes friend, Thor and I were old hands at coffee hours. Although they remained ordeals, we had worked out some survival techniques. It came down to two basic strategies. Under the first came the broad umbrella of medically sanctioned refusals relating to conditions ranging from ulcers and allergies to neurotic aversions.

Early on Thor had almost succeeded in the total abdication of responsibility through the simple expedient of stating, out of the blue, that he had a rare stomach ailment and his doctor had forbidden him all sweets. But having witnessed the consequences of my trying to eat for the family, he subsequently recanted, announcing just as precipitously that he had been healed—by a mysterious new drug. We agreed on equal time in the benefits from this recourse.

"And to think I have to pass up your lovely blueberry cream tart, " I lamented on one occasion, recounting a time I had survived on them during a camping weekend and now faced my stomach's indiscriminate rejection of them. One had, of course, to be extremely careful not to contradict oneself at a subsequent party.

As to our second stratagem, any diversion at a coffee hour was to be seized upon as an opportunity for furtive advantage taking. One didn't have to eat all of everything, and the size of things could be reduced by artful dissection. One looked for the smallest Viennese pastry or boldly asked for half of the one her husband took—on the legitimate ground that she covets it.

Fru Viborg's trip to the kitchen for a missing fork allowed me to lift a bit of icing to my plate and create an apparent space where none existed on the petit four service plate. During a spirited debate, Thor dissolved a creamed mint wafer in the remains of a second cup of coffee that he had no intention of drinking.

Once in awhile, after progressing past the halfway point along the table, Thor or I would simply state that we had had enough. That it was all so wonderful we had overindulged along the way.

"Just too big a piece of that magnificent ollalaberry cream cake, I guess," and let it go at that. But this was always an awkward business and was best reserved for the home of a woman whose entire board one had plowed through on a previous occasion. I had no remorse. My days were packed with enough coffee hours to turn me into a hippopotamus. And the route of honesty had been closed to us.

We were slowing down at R.I.P.'s. I had signaled Fru Viborg that, no thank-you, I was not quite ready for the pink bonbons. Fru Viborg passed the cigars and cigarettes, and the men lit up, marking the end of serious eating—although some sporadic picking through the nuts and candy bowl was to be expected.

Our hostess struck a large match to the fat cigar she had abandoned before dinner, and I decided to keep her company. I reached for one from the silver tray in front of me. By now I could manage the big cigars with aplomb and there was a certain defensive advantage, I had learned, in meeting smoke with smoke rather than simply expiring on the receiving end.

Our glasses were filled with icy aquavit, and R.I.P. lifted his studiously to the light. It appeared we were now going to have one of the pastor's famous anecdotes. "Rather an unfortunate tale, I'm afraid," he said.

Poor R.I.P.'s life, I knew, was plagued with small catastrophes which he seemed more adept at promoting than alleviating. He attracted disaster like a picnic lunch attracted the nearest ant colony. In an apparent attempt to reunite some quarreling couples, gossip had it that he had in one month precipitated two police calls and one general donnybrook, during which R.I.P. took the full impact of a skillet hurled by a muscular woman and intended for her drunken husband. The spectacle livened an otherwise uneventful winter week, and R.I.P.'s Sunday services enjoyed an uncommonly large attendance of villagers eager to see the great black eye which resulted from the drainage of the affected area and which lingered in shimmering colors of purple and gold.

"If the village doesn't get him off to do his research someplace, he's going to get himself killed," Thor said.

Now, true to form, his humor ran to the thanatological. "Did you know," he began, "that this house used to belong to a Swedish-born ragman and his wife?"

He had long before lapsed unapologetically into Danish. "That was years before it was remodeled as a parsonage. Well, the old Swede had bad feet and he came home one day suffering greatly, so his wife gave him the then-common home treatment, soaking his feet in rags dipped in aquavit."

"Aquavit?" I repeated.

"Oh yes," the pastor continued. "It is still regarded by many as an excellent medicament. Anyway, after the treatment was over, the old woman threw the bandages into the yard."

He hesitated, drawing deeply on his cigarette. "You may well imagine the old ragman's distress to awake the next morning and find the yard strewn with the limp and motionless bodies of their many geese."

"Good Lord!" said Herr Stenersen.

"Well," the pastor went on, "Swedes are a practical lot and the ragman and his wife plucked the geese of their feathers before tossing the bodies of the unfortunate animals on the dump heap."

R.I.P. surveyed us briefly before going on. "You can imagine their consternation when, hours later, they looked out to see the frantic activities of a dozen weird-looking creatures—the pink-skinned geese, denuded of feathers, not dead at all but wakened finally from their drunken slumber."

"Poor devils," Thor said.

"Oh, they are said to have made out very well," concluded R.I.P., who was tireless in his search for happy endings. "But,"

he added soberly, "with or without new feathers, I do not know."
It was a note to end on, and we took our cue.

Over the years I have developed my personal prognosticators
of impending minihorrors in whatever culture I find myself
launched into fieldwork.

Whatever waits out there, to be accommodated with inexorable
regularity: (1) it will be linked symbolically with all that is prized
in the culture; (2) circumvention of it will be antithetical to the
success of the proposed research; and (3) I will not be good at
it and/or it will make me sick.

12

Culture Shock
Trouble Along the Way

N
ature had found a new kind of fuss with which to enliven our hours, a three-day windstorm extraordinary even for Taarnby. From beyond the frozen harbor, water was driven out of the sound into the village streets, where it turned to an icy extension of the sea. And no one ventured out of the house.

We kept Katie home from school. Great gusts hit the house, which gave rumbling shudders with each assault, and the winds sucked the heat up our damperless *kakkelovn*. We decided finally, to chance the use of an electric heater we'd bought, despite our fears about the house's makeshift wiring.

That night I lay awake, listening for the wind's next pounding and listening harder for sounds of distress from the heater, which cast a wide band of orange light across the bedroom. The children slept. But I knew Thor was awake too. Once he got up and went down to check on the stove.

"Out cold," he said when he came up the ladder, "not an ash glowing."

We chafed at the loss of field time. It was difficult to get any work done at all with Katie and Sarah active and confined. And there was so much to accomplish. We were forever confronting what we called the "if onlys."

"If only the winter would break," Thor said at least once a day, staring out at the sound, which was still ice-locked. We watched the skies, waiting for the band of orange light to broaden.

"If only we could stay through another summer," I wished aloud.

If only the anthropological insights that were now so apparent had been swifter coming. The more we learned, the more we realized what remained to be done if we were to flesh out the solid ethnographic account of culture change that we wanted. Even after the windstorm had blown itself beyond the island and the streets were again navigable, we had trouble getting back into productive stride. Moments of self-doubt were more frequent, especially for Thor, who started waking at four in the morning, unable to fall asleep again. Some days he would be gray with fatigue by noon.

Sarah, who was growing fast, and whose happy antics attracted streams of children, was demanding more of my time. The house filled with children, who stomped in unannounced with snowy boots and blasts of arctic air and hovered over Sarah with damp clothes and trickly wet noses until I put a halt to visiting hours. Some days I would glimpse a face or two at the window, where the girls stood on upturned boxes to watch me bathe her. I would feel like an ogre. More and more frequently, frustration and a clinging sense of inadequacy would surge through me like pain. And Katie the intrepid would look at me and somehow understand and sit beside me, stroking Sarah's wisps of red-brown hair. Then I longed for home and help.

In later years, in a half-dozen other countries, we would come to recognize the symptoms, for they are common enough in fieldwork to have been given a name: "culture shock," a syndrome experienced in one form or another by all anthropologists. Our attack was late in coming.

Culture shock may develop anywhere from a week to several months after a move to another culture. Men and women develop a demoralizing sense of inadequacy, of hovering between a familiar way of life, from which they are removed, and a new world to which they cannot really belong. Diplomats, peace corps workers, business people abroad, and even those tourists who get off the packaged routes experience culture shock.

Depending on many things, including one's temperament (Type A personalities are definitely at risk), sense of humor (which is likely to convert to an acid tongue), time, and luck, sooner or later, culture shock strikes. Professionals struggle with dark fears of failure too dreadful and damning to articulate.

Some form of crisis eventually peaks, and either it is passed successfully or the sufferer throws in the towel and goes home. For the anthropologist, there is nothing ever so engulfing again as first culture shock.

Perhaps it was because Thor and I were so much together that we evaded the full syndrome for as long as we did. Love provided a kind of tunnel vision, locking us into a special and private world. However, when culture shock did hit, it was like getting the mumps at seventeen, not seven. Devastating.

What the weather didn't frustrate, we did. There were ten days during which we could do nothing right, and wound up wondering if we hadn't really hopelessly botched the whole damn Taarnby project. Nor did we recognize these frustrations for what they were, the deepest phase of culture shock.

And then, one afternoon when the children were napping, our Canadian friend, Tove, pounded on our door and came in with a basketful of hot doughnuts. Doors were rarely locked in Taarnby, and no one ever waited for us to let them in.

We had dubbed Tove, whom we loved, the anti-Betty Crocker of Denmark. She baked unrelievedly and wretchedly. The scent of the doughnuts alone was enough to activate the stomach to a fight-or-flight posture. But on this day I welcomed her visit, and Thor made none of his usual moves of escape to the typewriter. I put on water for coffee, because eating was inevitable, and there was no chance of getting the doughnuts past the esophagus without some serious dunking.

"It's a terrible time," she said, "but it's better to perish on the street from cold than at home from boredom."

I remembered her taste for good whisky, and after the doughnuts, went to the cupboard for the bottle of Scotch we had bought duty free on the Swedish ferry. It was early for drinking but a day for it. Thor gave the *kakkelovn* a stir, and the old stove hummed with heat.

We sipped the whisky neat in the local fashion, and Tove sighed expansively.

"Comfort," I echoed. "I don't think there's anything wrong with me that a lovely week of comfort wouldn't cure." I was feeling the Scotch creeping through my tense body like anesthesia.

Tove sat there cupping the glass in her hand, and then, like someone who has remembered an unattended pot on the stove, abruptly banged the glass down on the tabletop. "Then why not have it!"

"Have what?" Thor asked.

"A week. Away from here. Away from the wind and the sea. There's no escaping the snow. But it's a darling place."

We were speaking English or I'd have thought I had experienced another major lapse in my Danish. "What's a darling place?" I asked.

"My brother's house on Fyn," she said. "One large room with a kind of mezzanine that you get to by one of those iron staircases, all twisted like a snail. There's a great bed up there, almost the width of the room, built out of cedar like the house. All very modern with furry white rugs and a huge fireplace."

She turned to Thor. "That's Mons. He's an illustrator of children's books, and he has to go to Berne to work with an editor. He's begging me to come up and keep an eye on his house."

"Tove, you must go," I said. "We'll keep an eye on things here."

"With *Fastelavn* less than three weeks off?" Tove said, appalled. "As it is, I don't know if I'll get all my baking done."

Fastelavn (Shrovetide) is Denmark's equivalent of Mardi Gras, a time of pageantry for the village, a time when certain houses are visited by revelers who make their traditional visit from the neighboring community of Store Skive in the elaborate costumes of the nineteenth century's landed aristocracy. Tove's house, which bordered the beach, would be among those at which the mounted visitors made one of their ritualized stops for food and drink. She had talked of little else for weeks.

"What if there's snow?" I asked. "Will they have it if there's snow?"

"There will be no snow," Tove pontificated.

Thor laughed. "It's true," he said. "It's in the rule books somewhere." But then his face sobered. "Tove, thank you for a gracious and mighty attractive offer. But time is running out for us, too. We can't leave our work."

But Tove would have none of it. She told Thor to think of me, to think of Katie, to think of Mons. She had a charming pattern of nonstop speech, graphic with gestures, like an imperfect actress enjoying her moment on the stage. But she was quite earnest. "Say you'll think about it," she directed.

"We'll think about it," Thor said.

I was pouring us another whisky. Suddenly a bright and glorious light seemed to explode within my brain, illuminating its dark and troubled recesses. The way ahead lay before me as clear and appealing as the yellow brick road.

"Superfluous!" I said, raising my glass with a flourish. "Further thought is entirely superfluous!" For it was suddenly obvious to me that we couldn't not go.

Thor read my mind. I was transparent enough, smiling with beatific acceptance of this gift from the gods. I filled Tove's glass, and she clinked it against mine.

"Hold it! Hold it!" Thor protested. "We won't get a thing done."

"Not a thing," I said. "Not one typed note. Not an interview."

"It's way off to hell and gone," said Thor.

"In Denmark nothing's that far away," Tove countered.

"The roads are probably closed."

"Open," Tove advised. "Mons phoned today."

"Oh God!" said Thor, flinging his arms helplessly to his sides, palm out like some stricken saint. He stood there uncertainly, but—I could see—tempted now in spite of himself, in spite of the enormity of a week without a schedule, even a frustrated schedule.

"Think of it as therapeutic," I offered. "When we get back we'll more than make up for it." I meant it with an earnestness that made Thor look at me. His mouth and eyes lifted in a slow-spreading grin.

"O.K., Doc," he said. "O.K.."

"We're going?"

"Wouldn't have it any other way."

I couldn't bear the excitement of it. We were going to the Isle of Fyn. I ran to the front door and flung it open and yelled: "We're going to Fyn! We're going to Fyn!"

The wind howled and the snow swirled into the hallway. I stepped back into the house and Thor raced to close the heavy door, turning to face me. "Not if they lock you up first."

Tove took off to write Mons. "That way there's no turning back."

Katie surprised us by not wanting to go.

Although she wouldn't admit it, I knew she enjoyed her "little general" image in the community. She loved moving about the village, keeping track of things, roaming in and out of houses, waiting for the day when play groups could be organized outdoors again. She would peer out of our windows or hang over the gate, checking to see if there was ship activity on the vast Sound. Above all, she was waiting for the moment when the harbor ice sheet would show its first cracking, when the predicted patches of dark blue water would be visible again.

It was an event to behold, the seamen had told her, and the dreadful possibility that she might miss it, might not be among those to witness it firsthand, to spread the word to the less fortunate — this was too awful a contingency to dwell upon. Not even for a house with white fur rugs and a bed as wide as a room.

I was afraid she would regret her decision after we'd left. "No way, no way!" she said, slashing the air in front of her with her arms. "Besides, Tove is going to pickle herring in small jars and I get to put on the labels."

Katie could survive on pickled herring, one of her all-time favorite foods. And finally, she reminded me with suitable gravity, she could scarcely abandon Franz, housebound with tonsillitis, who looked forward to their lotto games. Ministrations to the sick were also among her running obligations in the village. I had to concede that for a six-year-old she carried some heavy burdens.

So we spent two days typing up the last of our untranscribed field notes, organized and posted the Schedule for the week of our return — activities which provided suitable balm for Thor's vaguely protesting conscience, and on a Monday took off for Mons's.

Our departures were somehow always complex productions, and this exodus was no exception. Thrilled to be carrying her own suitcase, which she packed herself, Katie insisted on walking to Franz's, from whose mother she had conned an invitation for the night. The rest of the week she would spend at Fru Odstadt's, whose fisherman husband had promised to show her how to mend nets.

Leaving Katie was like leaving a junior anthropologist in residence. As I would be reminded in subsequent fieldwork, children move with casual acceptance in worlds denied their parents. I often had to resist pumping Katie for information. For the most part, I respected her right to her world. Nevertheless, by the time we returned, Katie, I knew, would insist on sharing— with total recall—the major events of our lost week.

Now, when I saw her walk away, her suitcase firmly in hand, the yellow tassel on her hat swinging rhythmically from side to side, and watched her disappear in the vaporous half-light of morning, I burst into tears.

"It's two blocks," Thor said soothingly holding me. "We'll make sure she gets in."

"She's so small," I sobbed.

"So was Napoleon," Thor said, and I felt the laughter and joy rise up in me again.

Layered in wool knits and wrapped in shawls, Sarah's winter bulk filled her carrying basket, which Thor wedged securely into the back seat of our VW. A good traveler, Sarah loved the motion of the car and would soon be fast asleep. In the car's trunk were food, changes of clothes for Thor and me, and a large pile of diapers.

"Everything else," Tove had insisted, snatching towels from my hands, "will be at Mons's."

One mission remained.

Tove, her enthusiasm for our trip matched only by her pride in having initiated it, was making sure that the gesture did not go unremarked in the village. She had suggested that enroute we should deliver Fru Elgaard's eleven-year-old daughter to a community west of Copenhagen, where she might enjoy a long-postponed visit with a favorite and ailing aunt.

"Glad to do it," Thor said. "We can pick her up on our return trip."

It was natural and just that Tove should luxuriate in the public recognition of her enterprising spirit. Besides, Hilde was a sweet child, and we had pleasant and kindly feelings about being able to make this gesture to the family. Nevertheless, Tove's eyes still gleamed with the fires of invention, and we were eager to get on the road before her next entrepreneurial breakthrough.

If there is an axiom applicable to fieldwork in general it is that the worst troubles will arise in the least probable contexts. Our route to Fyn was not to be a smooth one.

We stopped in front of the Elgaard cottage, and Fru Elgaard emerged with Hilde in tow before Thor had turned off the ignition. Hilde looked strained and strange in "city clothes," as they were called in the village. She was wearing a slightly outgrown rough wool suit whose thickness probably made up for three layers of country challis. Hilde seemed pale and anxious. Something turned over inside me, and I felt the first unaccountable pang of fear.

Hilde's mother smiled fixedly at the child as the usual long-winded civilities were exchanged. And when discussion turned to the trip ahead, her eyes returned again and again to Hilde. "She's not used to being away from home," she said.

Thor said assuring things and I nodded vigorously from the car. Hilde stood beside her mother waiting for dismissal. "You will have a good time," her mother said at last.

"Of course, she will," Thor said, taking the cue and guiding Hilde toward the car, his hand between her shoulders.

"You will not cause any trouble to Doktor and Fru Anderson," her mother said. Smiling still.

"Of course she won't," Thor said, at his amiable best. He pushed the driver's seat forward. "Hilde, we have a special place for you in the back, right next to Sarah."

"You will greet your aunt from the family." A stylized admonition. Not a word from Hilde.

Thor started up the engine, sliding his long legs under the wheel. Fru Elgaard poked her head into the car through the open door. "Goodbye," I said.

"You will not disturb the baby." Her mouth was alongside Thor's ear. The car began rolling gently forward. "You will remember all the things I have told you." Fru Elgaard had gone into a kind of sideways canter.

Thor looked at me uncertainly. "You will close the door," I said in English as the car rolled gently around the corner, thereby disengaging itself from Fru Elgaard.

It wasn't until we were on the mainland and I experienced the comfortable vista of flat fields and spare trees that I turned to look at Hilde. Her eyes were open and focused on the car's ceiling. She seemed no more relaxed than when she had gotten into the car.

"You're missing the fields and, look!" I said. "There's a bird walking across that icy pond."

She moved her head briefly. And then turned her attention back to the roof of the car.

I nudged Thor. He looked in the rearview mirror at her. Then he shrugged.

We drove along in silence. The car was warming up and it felt good. Taarnby was behind us and lovely idleness lay ahead. Thirty or forty miles and we would deliver Hilde to her aunt and the world would become our private place. I could have purred. How long had it been since we'd had time alone together.

It occurred to me that we had done a wise thing, putting Taarnby behind us for a while. I could almost feel my brain being vacuumed of all the debris complicating our progress in our fieldwork. We were in good shape really. Very good shape. We'd come back, Thor and I, with a fresh vision of what remained to be done.

The planted roadside trees zipped past in pristine barrenness at regular five-second intervals, and I was about to remark on that fact to Thor, when I felt Hilde's tight grip on the side of my neck. "Stop the car, please!"

The urgency was unmistakable, and she was around me and out of the car before Thor had pulled fully off the road and nestled the VW against the banked snow. I went to her. Thor turned off the engine. Hilde had gone from merely pale to a decisive green.

"It's all right, dear," I said. "It's the excitement."

Thor brought a wad of paper towels from the trunk and a jug of water. "She'll be okay. I guess breakfast didn't sit very well."

"I didn't have any breakfast."

"We looked at one another. We were both seeing Fru Elgaard and the frenetic departure. The car was on the road, and I was getting nervous about Sarah. We got Hilde to rinse her mouth and walked her back the few feet to the car. She said she felt all right now, but she didn't look all right, except that she wasn't green any more.

The door was open on the road side and the interior had gotten very cold. Hilde climbed into the back and Thor started up, shifting into gear in slow motion. After a few hundred feet I turned around and asked Hilde how she felt.

"I'm fine now," she said.

We gradually picked up speed, and I got out the map. Thor read my mind. "Thirty-five miles."

I looked at the odometer. Ten minutes passed and then fifteen, and when I looked around again Hilde's head had found an apparently comfortable spot on the side of the car between the window and the back of the seat. Her eyes were closed.

I mouthed the word to Thor: "Sleeping."

He gave me an expansive smile just as Hilde's hand found the side of my neck again. I gave an involuntary cry and Thor jerked the steering wheel, stopping short of a plunge into a field. Sarah had been sufficiently jarred to cry, and I turned my attention to her while Thor raced after Hilde, who had disappeared behind one of the tarpaulin-covered mounds of cabbages common in the area.

In about five minutes he was back. "Same thing. Nothing coming up."

I looked out toward the field.

"She wants a minute or two," Thor said.

He adjusted Sarah's basket and took a rattle out of the glove compartment and shook it in front of her. She was settling down again. I went out and walked Hilde back with my arm around her. She said again she felt fine.

I thought she might be more comfortable in the front seat, but Thor was afraid she might leap out if there were another episode, so we resumed our seating arrangement. We moved along the road like some lost appendage to a funeral procession. By now the rearview mirror was adjusted to Hilde's face, and when Thor's eyes left it mine took up the watch. I have been more relaxed in a dentist's chair.

We made two more stops in less than ten miles. Finally, after we'd gotten Hilde settled for the fourth time, I signaled to Thor that we should talk. We moved around to the back of the car on the pretense of adjusting the luggage.

I had finally figured it out. How could we have been so dense! I leaned very close to Thor.

"Appendicitis," I said in a low voice.

"Appendicitis!" Thor yelled.

"For God's sake!"

"She has no pain," he mumbled. "No pain."

"She *says* she has no pain."

He thought about that and then darted toward the side door. I grabbed his coat.

"What are you going to do?"

"I'm going to feel her left side," he said. He stopped. "No, her right side."

"We're not going to feel anything. She's tense as a mousetrap as it is. She's clammy and pale and something is making her awfully sick." I hesitated. "We have to, to . . ."

"Hang on and get her to her aunt, I guess." Thor said.

"Her *sick* aunt, Thor. Her *sick, old* aunt."

He looked at me and his jaw sagged. "We have to take her back to Taarnby," he intoned.

"Oh Thor." I felt somehow sorrier for Thor than for little Hilde. I felt like some heartless torturer who had taken her victim off the rack only to push him, in an unguarded moment, into the alligator pit. Thor hadn't wanted this trip.

It took us almost two hours to retrace the miles and get out to Taarnby. Hilde was in and out of the car all the way back. When we rolled into the village it was like reappearing on the dock from which your cruise ship has just sailed. We drove stalwartly past a dozen houses whose windows, I knew, were manned by able observers who would rush to spread the astonishing news that we were somehow back. ("How can that be?" "I don't know, but I tell you I saw it with my own eyes—driving along the harbor road.")

Thor cut the engine as he pulled the car to the edge of the cobbled street. As in most of Taarnby, there was no sidewalk; only the recessed doorway to demarcate the entrance to Hilde's house.

Thor got out and I turned my attention to Hilde, tucking her hair under her cap, and wiping her face again. She was moist with perspiration. Fru Elgaard would be frantic. Thor's hand was on the knocker when the door opened. Fru Elgaard moved past him, wrapped her apron around her hands (an automatic gesture for protection against the cold), and stood a yard from me while I maneuvered Hilde out of the car. "So," she said. Her mouth lifted in the familiar unanimated smile.

I didn't know what to do. Thor did. He began in his most formal and precise Danish. "You should know that something of moment has occurred. You should know that we bring you unwelcome news, and that we are very sorry but your daughter is, ah, unwell."

He was losing his verbal stride, but he plunged on. "She is getting sick to her stomach every ten minutes, and one wonders if it is not indeed, though one hopes it will not be . . ."

And he finally got out the word.

"Appendicitis."

Fru Elgaard shifted her gaze from Thor to stare at me. Then she turned back to Thor again. "No," she said. She said it flatly, as one might to a child who has provided a lengthy but inappropriate solution to an assigned problem.

She turned her attention to Hilde. "Same thing?"

I had been looking at Hilde too, anticipating a sweep of terror across her face, wishing we had been cleverer at protecting her from the suddenness of the revelation. But Hilde's visage exuded peace. A newfound tranquility. Fru Elgaard's words snapped my eyes back to her. Thor too was staring at her.

"Same thing," he repeated. "What do you mean, 'Same thing'?"

"Carsick. She is always carsick, this one." She said it jovially. Almost with a touch of pride. She was smiling at Hilde.

The words hung there, frozen as the sea in the incredulity of the revelation. And all caution went out of me. "You *knew* she got carsick."

"Oh yes!" Fru Elgaard said. "She has been that way since she was three years old. One can take her nowhere." She shook her head.

"You let us take her. You let us take her on this our first vacation since we've come here."

"And very generous of you indeed," said Fru Elgaard, her complacency untouched. "And of Tove." Giving recognition where recognition was due.

"Tove knew of Hilde's problem?"

"Oh, I don't think so."

Thor was functioning again. "What we are both wonderng, Fru Elgaard," he said, and there was nothing in his voice except a kind of awed curiosity, "is why you didn't tell us that she gets carsick."

"Oh," said Fru Elgaard patiently, "if I had told you that you would then not have taken her. And we keep wishing that the next time she will at last have outgrown this little trouble. And if that had been the case, well, she would have provided no difficulty to anyone, now would she?"

She looked at Thor with a curiosity of her own. "I suppose you had to stop every ten minutes," she added.

"Every ten minutes. Yes. She was very ill, Fru Elgaard."

"Well," she said with a heavy sigh, "it's not getting any better, is it? She's like my husband's mother." And then, looking at the sky, she smiled. "Now you really have to be on your way." She studied us reprimandingly. "You should use as much of the daylight hours as you can, you know. And I don't want you worrying about Hilde. She'll be herself again in a few minutes. Of that I'm sure. Then I'll get some food into her."

She took Thor's hand from his side and shook it briefly. And I stood there limply while she found mine. Then she disappeared into the house.

In the car Sarah's small grunts were changing to earnest cries of hunger. Thor's eyes were fixed still on the little doorway through which Fru Elgaard, with Hilde in tow, had amiably retreated.

"I believe she forgave us for failure to manage a cure," he said.

"I believe we've been had," I said. "And I believe that in the future I shall expend my anthropological energies working in some uncomplicated little African village. Or maybe the New Guinea highlands. Yes, New Guinea is beginning to look very attractive."

"Remarkable," Thor said absently, still mentally bonded on Fru Elgaard.

"Why don't I drive," I said. "Sarah can hold out until we get off Taarnby and we'll find some lunch."

Thor was moving around the car when the door to the cottage flew open and Fru Elgaard raced out. In her hand was a paper-wrapped bundle. "Two liverpaste sandwiches. On nice, fresh, dark bread," she said, plunking the bundle into Thor's hands. "Hilde can slow you down, can't she?"

And she was gone again.

It was ten at night when our headlights found the house with the cedar door and green paint and M for Mons on a homemade crest on the mailbox.

The inside smelled marvelously of wood, and a fire was laid on a hearth big enough to walk into. In front of it a low-slung leather sofa promised luxurious hours of flame watching. The only other furniture was a thick three-drawered chest, richly carved, and four stools which faced the counter of a well-appointed little kitchen.

Tove had not exaggerated. A great wooden bed filled the mezzanine and was covered with a furry white throw.

I changed and fed Sarah and played with her while Thor removed one of the deep drawers from the chest, lined it with a blanket, and positioned Sarah comfortably within it, warm and sheltered. After a while we settled down for hot mugs of soup in front of the fire.

"What are you thinking?" Thor said. The firelight enveloped us in a rosy haze that touched the walls and made the whole room glow.

"I was thinking saintly thoughts," I said.

"For instance?"

"For instance, I forgave Fru Elgaard."

"Really?"

"Yes. I saw her head in the flames for awhile, but she kept on smiling. So I thought, what the hell! And besides, I'm too happy."

"Me too." Thor's voice was trailing off.

"Also, Thor . . ."

"Uh-huh."

"I was thinking perhaps I wouldn't leave for Africa or New Guinea just yet."

"Give it a week," he said, and turned off the lights.

And in a little while we went upstairs.

13

Celebration and Challenge

The Goose Girl

W hen we returned to Taarnby and the Schedule, it was to a village that had shrugged itself free of the worst of the snow and ice.

Katie was garrulous with news. We had missed everything. The very day we left, Anna (the "Sherman Tank") had fallen through the ice while skating near the geese reserve where sea water is blown in during the fierce winter months.

"She cut her lip," Katie recounted, "and when she saw the blood her face went all white and Herr Mygdal had to crunch through the water and ice and drag her from the spot."

Fru Nicolaisen had been the first to hang wash out-of-doors since the snow stopped: a bold but endearing move, for the first wash on the line was, more than the first robin, a true harbinger of spring. "But," Katie said, with suitable anguish, "it was too soon. Herr Nicolaisen's long drawers froze so hard they fell to the ground. And then there were two pieces. And Fru Nicolaisen had to sew the legs back together again."

Katie saw them in their hardened state.

"You could stand each leg up all by itself like a big white pipe."

The ice broke in the harbor, the big main harbor. "And you missed it. Gosh Mom!"

She paused so that the enormity of our deprivation could be fully appreciated by us. Had we waived the opportunity to witness the disembarkation of Columbus and his crew from the Santa Maria, our discretionary wisdom would have been no more suspect.

"Before it cracked it made *noises*. And Herr Strunge came and got me at Fru Odstadt's like he promised. And we saw it. In Danish you call it an icequake," she continued, ingenuously instructive.

"And all of a sudden one of the ships' masts began to move and a big piece of ice slid right up the side of Herr Ronne's boat. Herr Strunge said that broken ice can wreck ships. Crush them to bits! But it didn't wreck Herr Ronne's boat. He was lucky."

We got a half-hour of her time. "I have to go back. I'm helping Tove. I take the cookies off the tray and get the trays clean for reloading. And then I have to decorate the cookies with special designs."

She began working her scarf back into place around her neck. "I left a whole two batches for cooling."

"Will we have the pleasure of your company at dinner?" Thor asked.

"Sure, Daddy," she said, and she was off.

"I'm glad we got our reservations in," I said to Thor.

"She's having a great time," he said. "I'm not sure we'll ever get her out of Taarnby." And then, pensively, "Or should."

On Fastelavn the farmers from Store Skive made their traditional ride into Taarnby, dressed up in silk hats and vests and mounted on horses beautifully decorated with pearl-trimmed reins, with flowers in their manes and ribbons woven into their braided tails. A four-piece band follows the riders, and at each stop an impromptu dance takes place, and the horsemen seek a partner from the local women who gather for the pageantry.

The next day belongs to the children, and Fastelavn takes on the patterns, if not the mystique, of our Halloween, as boys and girls appear at the door in fancy costumes, singing a little rhyme especially for the occasion and rattling a small box for coins. Katie wore a Dutch costume, and like the rest of the children she carried a sapling branch, denuded of leaves but lavishly decorated with homemade ornaments of paper and yarn— symbolic of the coming of spring.

The weather cooperated as Tove had promised, with a flawless, sun-warmed sky of deep sapphire. And Katie roamed, red-cheeked, with only a sweater under her costume (a hard-won concession), steering her troops through streets that had been well mapped with generous hostesses in mind—and which included most of Taarnby. For the village loves its children and had been planning for days for their enjoyment and feeding.

Thor and I were kept busy observing and documenting all phases of the festivities.

There is a truism in anthropological research: that the final three months of fieldwork are more productive than the previous nine months combined. The end is in sight, and with it the prospect that you will soon be permanently distanced from your field site. Unanswered questions must then remain unanswered, short of the devastating cost of a return trip. This prospect had Thor and me piling up interviews, digging out data, and waking at 4:00 A.M. clutching the bedsheets, reviewing endlessly an extendable list of things undone.

This driven condition was one I approached sooner than Thor. Thor was given to steady states. Except for our joint plunge into late-blooming culture shock, a condition now behind us both, Thor was a born producer. He was organized and visionary, and I envied him. An inner sense of programming guided his footsteps through the village like the ordered rhythm of a Sousa march. I functioned differently, given to periods of inspired intensity, followed by a more relaxed productivity. Sometimes I had a comforting sense of control. But often I coveted Thor's professionalism and experience. I longed to have my neophyte status and first fieldwork behind me.

Part of it was personality, part of it legitimate differences in field style. It would be a while before I discovered that a broad range of approaches exists within which fieldwork can get ably done. The pace of fieldwork, the resiliency of the investigator, the sanctity accorded established priorities—all these vary with the individual and with the research project.

"One whole year"—as I had referred to the time allotted us— seemed initially a claim on eternity, particularly in the shapelessness of our first days in Taarnby. But now, looking back

over the months, time had shrunk like a cheap cotton shirt. And
we had work to do.

When Thor asked me to help with the photography for the
book, I was excited. We lacked candid shots that showed village
life in action and brought people into focus. I would do these
candid photos. Now that villagers were outdoors more routinely,
I had only to move about, alert for the right opportunity. I
developed a modified shoot-from-the-hip technique with my
camera that drew appreciative comments from subjects awed by
my footwork.

The precision involved gave me a lovely and alien sense of
command. I would wait patiently for the developed film to be
delivered from Copenhagen by Einar, our mailman, who rode
a gleaming bicycle and was resplendent in a red uniform with
wide polished belt and handsome cap on which was affixed the
crest of the Danish royal house.

Finally Thor was ready to call a halt to the photography. "We
have everything we wanted, haven't we?"

"Almost everything," I told him. Three things still eluded me,
two of which, I was quick to argue, would enhance the book.

"First of all, I want a couple of pictures of the geese," I said.

Every morning the geese made their way through the streets
to the village greens, where they fed and where their eggs were
gathered for sale or incubation. Various flocks would come
surging down the untrafficked lanes, briefly disperse at a
crossroad, only to refunnel into the narrowing cobblestones of
the next block, stampeding one another in clumsy haste. Here
and there a crowded beast would spread its heavy wings and
make unmelodic and raucous sounds, for they were known as
ill-tempered creatures and sometimes struck out menacingly with
their beaks.

But geese were distinctive of Taarnby, a familiar and flamboyant
sight, with their passage filling the space between the cottages
like a feathered avalanche. I had experienced bad luck in finding
a locale where I might be in front of them but not overrun by
them in their sweep through town. The truth was that I liked
them not at all and was more than a little afraid of them. But
photographing them had become a challenge.

"Second," I told Thor, "I want a shot of someone swimming
off one of the beaches."

"Swimming?" Thor said. "Who'd be swimming?"

"Well, Tove says some of the more intrepid take to the waves as soon as the water warms up."

"My God," Thor said.

Since in mid-August the water could turn your ankles to a raw, purple-red in ten seconds, the residents' expectation of significantly warmer water in spring was idiocy on the face of it. But nevertheless, by mid-July boys and girls would be hurling themselves into the sea with abandon.

"Should have gotten it when we came," Thor said intelligently.

But we hadn't gotten it. "Besides," I told him, "it would really be something to get a picture of a single swimmer with a sweep of the sea and perhaps a fishing boat behind him. Very thematic. The timeless sea of old Taarnby. The solitary man taking on the primordial elements with exuberant enthusiasm. It would make a stunning book jacket, Thor."

"And plunge some hapless idiot into heart failure." He shrugged, unimpressed. And we left it there. When I could, I hovered about the harbor, hoping—in vain—for the appearance of the phantom swimmer.

About the third unrealized photograph I did not unburden myself to Thor. Nor had I committed myself to a definite course of action. But thoughts of it were at the perking stage.

Since our first days in Taarnby, I had been intrigued with tales of the tømmer, and now I had gotten it into my head that his photo should properly be included in our proposed gallery of village occupations. The tømmer was the man who came in the middle of the night with his horse-drawn cart and serviced the outhouses, capping and replacing the five-gallon vats that slid from their cabinets beneath the seat and carrying his loads to sewage disposal areas far from the village.

He moved through the streets with noiseless efficiency, and a complex lore had built up about him. He was variously reported to be a former member of the foreign legion whose throat had been cut in an Arab war so that he was mute, or an eminent brain surgeon whose life had fallen apart when his wife left him for some blackguard; or it was a woman, powerful and solitary of mood, who lived in a tidy cottage on the other side of the island. Whoever it was, he or she was oddly respected as punctilious in manner and scholarly of mind, though how that consensus had been reached no one could say.

I felt that a photograph that lifted the *tømmer's* activities from the unfortunate obscurity that surrounded them was definitely in order.

The time had come, I decided, for the countdown: first a photo of the geese, then of the swimmer, and finally a try for the *tømmer* if I could figure out a way to do it without embarrassment.

Katie would be my best resource on the geese. And sure enough, she came charging into the house on a Saturday morning.

"Geese! Maybe thirty of them."

"Where?"

"Bearing down on the courtyard in front of the widow Ina's."

I knew the spot. The odd-shaped frontage forced traffic into the twisting neck of a street that was too narrow for automobiles and that would now funnel the peripatetic geese past our door. No doubt about it!

It was 7:00 A.M. Katie had been out on her usual weekend dawn patrol. I had just nursed Sarah and was boiling water for coffee. Thor was upstairs sleeping. He had been at the town meeting until after eleven, and I had heard the typewriter still clicking away downstairs at one in the morning.

Even with the milder spring weather, our cement-floored kitchen was tomb cold, and I was in *mukluks*, leather-soled heavy woolen socks, and a flannel nightgown whose voluminous bulk created comfortable weight right down to my insteps. But for propriety's sake I wanted my robe, and my camera.

"Mom! hurry!" Katie remonstrated and ran outside again.

Those geese really traveled when they got going. And the narrow lane after the wide courtyard would have provoked a stampede and pandemonium. I could get a shot of them in magnificent animation, white wings flashing. But it would be like positioning oneself before the floodwaters of a broken dam. I needed all the time I could get. I needed to get out on that street.

My robe was upstairs. Forget it, I decided. Who'd be out there at 7:00 A.M. anyway? All I needed was a few seconds. I moved Sarah from the highchair to her crib, grabbed my camera from the desk, and headed out the Dutch door into the yard just in time to see Katie's head bobbing up and down beyond the gate which—together with our rough-boarded fence—separated the garden and the outhouse building from the street and, at this moment, from the oncoming geese.

"They're in front of Fru Odegaard's," Katie yelled.

How could that be! Fru Odegaard was on our block. Those animals must be jet-propelled. And sure enough, as I opened the gate I could see them, wall-to-wall white down feathers, their myriad necks emerging from a sea of white as though they were one monstrous creature, a wretched mutation venting its wrath upon the earth, consuming its way through a hapless sea village. Geese obscured every cobblestone, and their mass seemed to slide up one house wall briefly, only to swish suddenly to the opposite side of the lane to the accompaniment of high-pitched squeals from those geese most pressed against. Their wings unfurled in leaping whiteness.

I slung the camera around my neck and checked the focus and the speed. As I did so, I caught the top of Katie's hat through the lens.

"Katie," I called.

"Come on, Mom," she said, urgency in her voice.

I wanted her inside the gate, not outside it. I realized now that I could get my picture from inside the garden. The fence was low enough. There was enough curve in the street to allow for a great shot. But first I wanted Katie off the street.

I flung open the gate just as Katie made her move to the safety of the pilot's yard across from ours.

"Shoot mom, shoot!" she called.

I got down on one knee in the street. But by then it was like focusing on the middle of a king-sized white sheet. The geese were now too close. Certainly too close for comfort. I took the shot and leaped toward the gate.

I made it at the same time the geese did, exploding into the yard around me. It was as though some giant hand was hurling them through the open gate in sets of two or three. They would come through airborne, trying to bring their spread wings into collapsed position as they landed around me, only to pick themselves up and hurl themselves in their panic against the wall on the far side of the garden, wings opening again. For the first time I made eye-to-eye contact with one of them and felt the brush of a firm, horny, open beak. Another hit me sideways with her remarkably firm broad body.

All that occurred in the seconds it took me to turn and slam the gate shut before the remaining half of the flock could follow. I gave the heavy gate a healthy shove, pushing it with the extended fingers of one hand—which was as close as I could get to it. Immediately there followed a shriek, louder than the rest and alarmingly human. It was emitted by an animal caught in the nearly closed gate, whose body was outside and whose head was inside the garden. I half expected the head with its bulging eyes to drop from the very long neck which, when I released my pressure on the gate, seemed to extend itself to that of an ostrich. But the goose merely gave a spasmodic lunge, squeezed through the gate, and, obviously shaken, began a careening dance around the yard.

I still held my post at the gate, pushing now against the growing weight of the bodies and shoving an assortment of goose appendages from the inside to the outside of the garden. One animal nipped at my hand with serious intent, drawing the flattened palm into its beak. I made a fist of my other hand and struck her soundly on top of the head, in response to which she released my hand, only to grab the hem of my gown just as the garden gate closed firmly shut on it and the inside latch fell into place.

As the animal distanced herself from the gate, my nightgown began to rise, twisting into a tight mass that reduced my mobility to a hobble.

In the meantime, the badly choreographed ballet continued as flat-footed geese pirouetted about the garden, racing back and forth through one another's ranks. Once in awhile one of them would sail past me, but their energies were wholly directed toward getting out of there—a course of action I heartily supported but was now at pains to assist.

"Hey Mom!"

"No, Katie! No!" I yelled, afraid she would enter the garden. If those creatures could take me hostage in my own yard, think what they could do to a little child.

"Hey Mom!" Katie called again. And the gate opened, plunging the goose with the hem of my nightgown in her beak precipitously across the garden, and twirling me to the ground on top of her.

Katie crowded alongside me, "Mom, you could hurt her," she said solicitously.

"My nightgown," I yelled. "The goddamned beast's got my goddamned nightgown."

"Just zonk her, Mom," Katie said, standing over me. "Just zonk her." And finally, "Like this, Mom!"

She walked up to face the goose who, erect now, had braced her wide-webbed yellow feet into the dirt, intent on pulling me and my nightgown firmly across the yard. Even with her neck bent, the goose came up to Katie's chin.

"See?" Against one side of the beak, Katie gave the goose a resounding snap of all four fingers, rapidly unfolded from a fist. Then she gave her a determined second snap on the other side of the beak. "Let go of my mother," she instructed.

The animal did forthwith, its sizable rump briefly hitting the flower bed as a consequence of the momentum generated in the release.

"That was not nice to do," Katie remonstrated, still addressing the animal.

She turned her attention to me. "How about a shot of me, shooing them out of the yard and down to the harbor," she said, with sudden inspiration.

And that's how she appeared in the photo, flourishing a switch which she tore from the apple tree in our garden, marshaling the geese into parade order and heading for the green. I had to crop from the photo the intrusive figures of the pilot and his wife, who by then were riveted to the spectacle from their position outside the gate of their own cottage. Herr Strunge still held a coffee spoon firmly in hand.

Thor, who slept through it all, was critical of the picture, which, he said looked staged.

"It isn't as though she were a *real* goose girl," he said.

I thought it close enough to accuracy.

14

An Ethical Issue
Shooting the Outhouse Man

thical issues are unremittingly a part of fieldwork. I don't
believe that any anthropologist who has spent any time
in the field has found herself unchallenged or untested.
Sometimes the right decision is evident; sometimes the issues
are murky.

I did not get a photograph of a swimmer in the waters of the
sound. I could find no one "bereft enough of reason," as Thor
put it, to be coaxed into the still-glacial waters. "Short of pushing
some hapless fisherman into the sea, I'd give up on the phantom
swimmer," Thor advised. And I did.

I was less willing to surrender on my plans for the *tømmer*.
In the challenge, I managed to succumb to the faulty but classic
rationale that the end justified the means. As it happened, I did
not get the photograph of our night visitor, although not because
of the failure of an ingenious scheme I devised to catch him in
action.

At the front of our cottage, triangular thatched eaves rather like
a tricorn hat hung over the heavy Dutch door. I climbed up there
one day to see if the birds were nesting in the hollow, as Katie
thought, but there was nothing. Nothing but leaves and debris
piled up thickly inside. My next informant was not due for forty
minutes, so I climbed down, got into a pair of jeans, returned
to the eaves and started cleaning them out.

Before I knew it, I was into the recess up to my waist. And
there was still room. I pulled myself all the way in and pivoted

around so as to face the garden. It was like being a child again in a backyard tree house. I had an extraordinary view of the sound. Directly below and in front of me was the roof that covered the outhouse and shed. The structure looked odd and alien from that angle.

Then, from my right, the red uniform of the postman came into sight. I saw Herr Ringe round the corner, ring the bicycle's bell at our gate, and after a couple of seconds, deposit the mail in our box. I watched him, my chin on my hands. He looked at the built-in ladder in front of which I had left a broom. His head tilted upward, but there was not the slightest flicker of recognition, no sign of his having seen me. He remounted his bicycle and sped away.

My eyes went to the shed again. How small it looked. Under that little roof lay on one side our wood and coal supply and on the other, the primitively simple accommodations of the outhouse. The next generation in Taarnby would not live with outhouses. The children of today's fishing and pilot families who were now routinely seeking employment in Copenhagen would demand and have indoor plumbing. The *tømmer*, along with other tradesmen whose activities were part of a disappearing way of life, would vanish too. The *tømmer's* old flat-topped cart and the shaggy workhorse that pulled it would not be heard in the dark village streets.

I sighed. Then laughed. Many a night I'd have pledged us all into indentured servitude for a lovely American toilet. Nevertheless, I really would have liked a photograph of the cart and the man who drove it.

I was maneuvering myself down the ladder when an idea whipped through my brain. I scurried back up to the top of the ladder and checked the camera angle. Magnificent! One couldn't ask for a better shot. From the eaves I could get the man, the shed, and the wagon complete with horse. In my prone position he'd never see me. I could take a photograph of the *tømmer* leaving the yard, back to the camera, protecting his identity. It was appropriate that his picture be in our book. We owed it to posterity.

I told no one. I was having considerable trouble with the ethics of what was taking firmer shape in my mind. But I got past that impasse by resolving that I would go to the *tømmer* and secure his agreement — once I got the shot.

For the next two weeks I monitored the *tømmer's* exact arrival time on his twice-weekly visits. I owned an enamel travel clock with a feeble alarm. Its gentle vibrations would do the trick. I placed it well under my pillow and set the alarm for 3:00 A.M., and on the first vigil waited a full hour, confident I had missed his visit.

There were only four stops for the *tømmer* on our street, and since he approached from the town and not the harbor, ours was the last house on his route. Then, in the noiseless night, I picked up the unmistakable rhythm of the hooves on the cobblestones. I took my clock from under the pillow and noted the time on its luminous dial.

The *tømmer* needed exactly twelve minutes from the moment the horse stopped at the top of our street until he reached the gate in our yard. Time enough for me to slip into my jacket and slacks, put on my tennis shoes, and with flashlight in hand and camera around my neck, move quietly downstairs, out the front door, and up the ladder.

I practiced the run until I was satisfied I could execute it expertly and silently in the allotted time. The fact that I would need to take a flash shot presented a separate challenge, and initially I thought I must abandon the idea of the photograph on that basis alone. However, as I lay in my lofty perch and watched the *tømmer* come and go, I figured out how I could do it.

The familiar garden took on an eerie dimension in the dead of night. Stretched out beside the dark, breathing sea, the whole village assumed an air of malevolence. The cobblestones glistened blackly as the moon moved in and out of hunchbacked clouds, working its way across the water to Sweden. It was a set for Frankenstein or for the sudden sweep of vampire bats.

When the gate opened and the dark-robed figure of the *tømmer* moved toward the shed below, my chest constricted in brief, irrational fear. But I made no sound as the *tømmer* went about his business. From the cart a beam of light rotated from a fixed lantern, flashing rhythmically on and off. Its beam was directed downward and was singularly bright.

I watched the *tømmer* disappear into the shed and replace the container through the hinged wooden panel beneath the seat.

Finally he closed the door of the shed, walked out of the garden, and lifted the container to the flatbed of the truck where others lay enclosed by a series of strategically placed and removable wooden posts.

Only then did he close the gate and climb back on his wagon, picking up the reins. The horse moved knowledgeably along without a gesture from the *tømmer*. Man and horse and the flashing light seemed to float out to sea, and the garden was plunged into darkness.

I observed the *tømmer* on two more occasions, and the routine was unvarying. He wore a coarse hat with a broad sloping brim and flaps that protected his ears from the wind and cold. A yellow rain slicker was visible on a hook beside his seat, but the weather held dry, and he wore a kind of poncho that—when he lifted his arms—made him look like a giant bat. There was never a sound from him. He didn't cough, or sneeze, or hum, or clear his throat, or address a word to the horse. It was like watching a kind of languid robot.

With the third vigil I had figured out how to get the photograph. I would synchronize my flash with the rhythmic flash from the rotating wagon light. Shot with precision, the brightness of my flash would go undetected, particularly if I took it at the moment when the *tømmer*, with the garden gate open behind him, turned his back to the house and his attention to the wagon.

I practiced, mastering the rhythm, with an empty camera. I could take only one shot and I should promptly have to make myself as invisible as possible in my hiding place. In any case, once the *tømmer* mounted the wagon seat, the risk of a second shot would be too great. When I learned that a full moon was imminent, I was galvanized into the decision to go forward with my plan. Although the additional moonlight posed a certain personal risk, it would diminish the impact of the flash.

However, Sarah had a colicky night, and I had to reschedule my photograph for the *tømmer's* second, rather than first, visit of the week. The moon was still bright. When I left the upstairs Sarah was snoring contently, her stomach calmed by Doktor Lars's ministrations and—I suspected—by the milk, honey, and brandy ("a little drop") that a solicitous Fru Odstadt had poured into her before bedtime.

I was now quite expert in settling into my perch. My heart, however, beat with excitement. Rehearsals were behind me. This was the real thing. I ran through my mental checklist. I had loaded and tested the camera, including the flash. The tømmer was on his way. I had heard the wagon, though the streets were silent now. He was at the widow Ina's. Next, old man Larsen. And then us.

Sure enough, in five minutes the first flash of the tømmer's light slashed low against the garden wall, and when the gate was opened the yard was thrown into bursts of dazzling whiteness.

I lifted myself to my elbows, positioned the camera to my eye, left index finger poised over the button that would trigger both the lens and the flash. I counted the slow one-two, one-two, one-two of the rotating lamp: one for darkness, two for the sweep of light. The tømmer entered the shed. One-two, one-two, one-two. Then he emerged. A moment to secure the door of the shed and his back would be toward me. When he opened the garden gate it would be time. I took a deep, careful breath and lifted my torso free and clear of the edge of the eaves.

And then, suddenly, it was as if I were witnessing the whole scene for the first time: the quiet tømmer and the gentle horse moving with dignity and purpose through the vacant night. And there I was hovering over them, calculating and intrusive. It was my presence, tucked under the eaves, which the night wrapped in shadow. Everything else lay before me with inviolate clarity. One two, one-two, and I couldn't move my finger. Then the moment was gone. The tømmer was on the wagon, and the horse, pale now in the moonlight, lifted his head erect and moved toward the sea.

I felt quite undone. As though at the last second I had moved from the train crossing, unaware until that moment of the danger that hurtled past me. How could I even have thought of taking the photograph? My judgment had been terribly wrong. It was a close call. And it was an experience that permanently shaped my awareness in field situations of the siren song of opportunity and the dreadful price of seduction by it. Ethical priorities are most at risk when the success of fieldwork seems to depend on the anthropologist's ability to justify compromise with them.

After awhile, I climbed down the ladder and went back to bed. It was a long time before, with a great unburdening sigh, I fell into a dreamless sleep.

15

Leaving the Field
Disaster and Deliverance

L eaving the field can offer as many challenges for the anthropologist as entering it. For Thor and me, practical and emotional issues competed for attention as, with the end of our work in Taarnby in sight, we took stock of our situation.

Our image of ourselves had come to be identified with village life and legitimized in our associations with Taarnby's men, women, and children. Despite some daily frustrations, our existence had taken on a predictable tempo. Now, the renewal of links with the outside world—a prospect we had dreamed of—developed a qualified appeal. Over the months in Taarnby, the villagers' suspicions of us had yielded to acceptance and, imperceptibly, on the part of our neighbors and informants, to real affection—an affection we reciprocated.

In the final days, our anxiety about departure mounted, though Thor and I seemed unwilling to discuss it or even acknowledge it, if indeed we were capable of verbalizing our discomfort.

"So, you are going, are you?" Tove said to me one afternoon, as I separated clothes to leave from clothes to take with us. "Going back to your real home."

I turned to stare at Tove. Tove, who in the purity of anthropological field vocabulary henceforth would assume a permanent identity among our "principal informants." Tove, who from the beginning had done so much to open the world of Taarnby to us. Friend and confidante, counselor and cook, Katie's fictive

133

second mother. The absurd thought came to me, and I held it briefly and fiercely, that we could not leave this place.

"I feel as though we are *leaving* home," I told Tove.

In Taarnby we had become part of a security network, and now at this moment in our lives there was for us precious little security to which to return. Six thousand miles from home, with grant funds winding down, we faced the almost certain prospect of arriving in the United States jobless. I was still a graduate student with a doctoral dissertation to write and was a long way from being marketable as an anthropologist. Thor had no university appointment and, realistically, no paid research prospects. We had chosen the field experience over job security at this point in Thor's career, and despite our mounting level of apprehension, we did not regret our decision to come to Taarnby.

I tried to be enterprising. While Thor had answered some "Assistant Professor Wanted" ads in the Anthropology Newsletter, I had been pursuing some of the more improbable opportunities described in the barrage of announcements from federal, state, and private agencies on whose mailing lists I had promoted us over the months in Taarnby.

"Inflicted us," Thor corrected one day when I came back from the mailbox with an assortment of official-looking envelopes. "The accumulated postage alone would be enough to keep us alive for a month."

"Nonsense," I said. "This is absolutely fascinating stuff. You don't know how qualified you are as an anthropologist. I'm going to apply for anything that could mean work. Trust me."

In addition to meeting a field schedule of ever-intensified interviewing, I was getting off an application a week for some kind of funding. In the process of this assembly-line approach to grantsmanship, I learned a great deal about Thor. He was not one-fourth Native American, not the descendant of a Confederate soldier, and not interested in becoming a specialist in swamp cultures. While the latter opportunity had dubious appeal, any one of these contingencies would have qualified him for rich sources of funding. I asked two separate federal agencies to let us replicate, in France (where I could speak the language), the culture change study we were completing in Taarnby.

But as the weeks passed, nothing materialized. It could be months before we would hear one way or the other about subsequent academic or research employment. I plugged on with applications and with fieldwork. Our workdays sometimes stretched to fourteen hours.

There were holes in various areas of collected data, and we suddenly became mindful that we had to do something about them or be ready to face whatever subsequent problems might arise when we were into the actual writing. We devoted a couple of nights to a lengthy annotated account of the scope of what was contained in those little five-by-eight inch cards. Actually we wound up with *two* written accounts. One allowed us to see how adequately we covered knowledge of Taarnby's past from an 1890 ethnographic baseline to the present. A second account looked to our still-viable table of contents for any significant gaps between what we proposed to cover in our book and what we were prepared, as of right now, to address. These subject areas would provide the various ethnological foci around which the culture change analysis would evolve. We wanted a supersaturation of field data. Information on Taarnby needed to be sufficiently broad and rich to allow maneuverability in our theoretical analysis of the dynamics of change over a half-century.

Sometimes we looked to be in very good, even excellent, shape. Then one of us would say: "Well, what if we decide we want to (there followed a range of stabs into future decision making) . . . can we handle that?" And we'd either find ourselves happily self-congratulatory because we certainly *could* handle that, or we would stare at one another reflectively if we came up with serious reservations.

Finally Thor wisely called a halt to it.

"We're loaded with data," he said. "We've worked like hell. We go with what we've got!"

You go with what you've got. A good dictum. Particularly if you come to terms with the realization that—fortunately—there is never a cutoff on cultural insights. Witness the potential of a single field site to attract some anthropologist to the intermittent study of it over a decade or more.

Nevertheless, neither Thor nor I could pass up opportunity. When Herr Wik's brother returned from a year in Holland, Thor met with him on three occasions. Peder, in his seventies, owned a collection of sketchbooks. A ship's chandler, he had an eye for detail and had acquired a useful gallery of harbor views, each of which chronicled some phase of Taarnby's maritime past. Grete, the cooking-school alumna, unearthed a book on child care published in 1912 and thumb-worn from family use. The discussion it provoked, particularly of a chapter entitled, "No Longer a Child," afforded lively and fruitful information on youthful dating patterns as well as engagement and marriage.

Two weeks before our scheduled June 15 departure from Taarnby, a birthday check arrived from my father in the lavish amount of one hundred dollars, and we threw a party. A fare-well party.

Katie went from door to door accompanied by her friend and shadow, Franz, reciting the invitation in the stilted and change-less fashion that had been used in the community for decades. "I should greet you from my parents, Herr Doktor and Fru Doktor Anderson, who respectfully invite your attendance at a party in our home at eight o'clock on May 24."

My German chocolate cake—put together from a mix sent by a fellow graduate student—was dubbed "Katie's mother's cake," and after the first forkful, women's heads snapped in my direction, their eyes fixed on me with a look as close to unqual-ified respect as I had experienced in eleven months of fieldwork. Fru Christensen approached me, cake in hand, patted my wrist, and then rather contritely murmured something to Thor. I raised my eyebrows inquiringly.

"'Still waters run deep,'" Thor said, when she had moved away, "or the Danish equivalent. I believe they think you've been gracious enough not to demonstrate your mastery of American cuisine until now."

Suddenly, it seemed, departure was less than a week away. What we couldn't get into our luggage we would pack into the Volkswagen to follow us via ship from Copenhagen. Included was Katie's purple scooter, from which, at the last moment, she decided she could not be parted.

Thor and I got passport identification for Sarah, and we went into Copenhagen to pay for the airline tickets and sign the papers for the shipment of the car. We had lunch in a chic restaurant in Stroget, Copenhagen's elegant shopping district, as a kind of private farewell to the capital. It was a fortunate decision in that it was the last food either of us would be interested in swallowing for the rest of the day.

At about two o'clock we entered our bank, and Thor expansively removed from his wallet the bank draft that Bernard, his father, had drawn on the last of our savings in the United States, a reserve which we must now use to get us and our possessions home. At the bank window was our regular teller, who over the year, had supervised the intricacies of depositing dollars and dispensing kroner. I felt childishly pleased to see Thor push so heroic a check across the counter.

The clerk picked it up and studied it with his usual stoicism. He was one of a strain of humorless Danes. "In traveler's checks, please," Thor said. "All of it."

I nudged him. "The account!"

"Oh yes. We'll want to close our account. We'd like that money in U.S. dollars." Thor smiled, savoring the moment. "We're going home."

The man smiled. And I had benign thoughts about this prosaic little man, who in personality was the least Dane-line person I'd met. "Yes, sir," he said. "Will you want your dollars now or on the day you come in for your traveler's checks? If you know what denominations you want, I can have them ready for you."

"Oh, we don't mind waiting," Thor said amiably. "As a matter of fact, we really need to get everything taken care of today."

There was a silence, during which I felt the first stab of apprehension.

"We will, of course, negotiate the draft with all dispatch," the man continued. "With luck we should be able to make the funds available to you in two weeks—barring unforeseen difficulties, of course. I should say it would be more realistic to keep three weeks in mind."

Thor's eyes met mine, then snapped back to fix on the teller. Thor seemed to grow perceptibly taller than his six feet. All amiability left him. "Will you tell me what in blazes you're talking about?" he said. "We need money to ship a car, pay for our airline tickets, and get out of Copenhagen in four days. You are holding an international bank draft. You are talking to customers who have maintained an account in your bank for almost a year. That bank draft is negotiable anywhere in the world!"

Our teller maintained a funereal calm, although his eyes had widened and he backed away from the counter as Thor's considerable bulk penetrated and filled the window. "It is negotiable at any bank listed as a formal receiver. Yes. Unfortunately . . . ." He spread his hands in a gesture of regret and finality, "this bank is not one of them."

"Could you tell us at which bank it *can* be honored?"

The man turned and from a shelf behind him extracted a thin volume. He drew a practiced finger down what was apparently an index and then turned his interest to the body of the book. On one page his finger found something of interest and he inserted a sheet of notepaper. Then, having turned to another page, he faced us spreading the open book on the counter. "You have two choices," he said, staring at the open page.

"Fine," said Thor.

The man cleared his throat. "They are at some distance, I'm afraid."

"No problem. We have a car." Thor took a pen from his pocket and ripped a sheet from the pad on the counter. Then he looked expectantly at the clerk. "Shoot!"

"First," said the clerk, "Credit Lyonnais, its central office, Paris. Then there's the British Bank of Commerce and Trust, London, which apparently also has a foreign department in its Liverpool branch. However, I would certainly check on that before presenting myself." He smiled knowledgeably at Thor, as though the vagaries of the British banking system were now the central issue.

It took perhaps ten seconds for the shock waves to work their way through our nervous systems, at which point Thor and I reacted simultaneously with an outburst that sent the clerk for administrative assistance "of the highest order."

It had been two o'clock when we entered the bank and after four when we shambled back through the lobby in defeat, like the pathetic remnants of some ill-conceived insurrection. We had talked to the manager, the director of overseas banking, and a vice-president, from whose office we made telephone calls to three other Copenhagen banks, to the American Embassy, and to American Express. The clerk was correct. The money had been sent in a form that tightly restricted its negotiation.

"We don't see many of these any more," the vice-president said, examining the draft as one might examine a Confederate dollar. "If it had been in the name of this bank, but . . ."

But whatever it was supposed to have been, it wasn't. At last I led Thor from the bank. He was in deepest shock. "I simply don't understand it. How could my father have sent such a thing?"

I steered him in the direction of the Hotel d'Angleterre. "He didn't know," I said.

"No, no. I told him to go to my bank. That draft was not issued by my bank."

We had surrendered the draft to the vice-president for processing through the Paris bank. American Express would willingly provide us with some cash, but not enough to pay for the airline tickets, nor could we charge them, for that would take us over our approved credit level. The American Embassy, our final recourse, advised cabling our next of kin of our plight — which we chose not to do.

"Where are we going?" Thor queried as we crossed the pigeon-filled square beyond Strøget.

"To the bar at the Hotel d'Angleterre."

We had two rounds of very expensive whisky. Thor's color was coming back. "What the hell," he said.

"What the hell," I intoned.

We agreed to say nothing of the turn of events, and at five o'clock we headed disconsolately back to Taarnby. Our cottage was to be repossessed in five days, and there was no alternative housing to be had in the village. We decided that when the day came we would leave Taarnby as scheduled and hole up somewhere in Copenhagen until the draft had gone through channels.

I finished our packing except for the few kitchen things we might continue to need and which I had intended to leave for Tove. But now I set aside two suitcases for the Copenhagen layover and rescued an old duffel bag of Thor's to stuff with diapers and bottles for Sarah. In standard field procedure, Thor and I sorted out the duplicates of our final field notes for shipping by mail to the United States.

The next morning Katie left for school, and Thor headed for Copenhagen to find a place for us to stay until our cash came through. At eleven o'clock there was a knock on the door, and outside was Herr Ringe with a telegram in his hand.

No one had awarded us a twenty thousand dollar grant — my first wild thought. Instead a message from the vice-president of our Copenhagen bank read:

> French mail and phone strike. All communications delayed.
> Advise immediately on disposition your bank draft.

Thor returned at four o'clock. Katie was home, and he said nothing of Copenhagen. But as I watched him thrash around the living room, I knew that the news was not good.

When Katie left, cupcake in hand, for Franz's, Thor flung himself into a chair. "You won't believe it."

"Yes I will."

"I went everywhere. Agencies, hotels, newspaper ads. I even went to the housing office at the university. The timing's rotten. Everything's sewn up for the summer people."

He pulled out a notebook and began flipping through some pages. "What there is is wildly expensive, even in the suburbs. Without a lease it's just about impossible anyway."

He hesitated. "There is a little hotel that Bjorn at the university put me onto. Clean and simple with continental breakfast."

"We can handle that," I smiled.

"With the special weekly rate it comes to almost three hundred dollars for two weeks. After that we go into summer rates, which are thirty percent higher."

"Three hundred dollars!"

We couldn't handle that. And there'd be our meals. And what if the time dragged on? I remembered the telegram. I couldn't bring myself to tell Thor about the telegram. Not yet.

Thor snapped the notebook shut. "Something might break. We have a couple of days." He looked thoroughly drained.

I got up to pour us both a drink.

"Three hundred dollars!" Thor repeated. He tossed the notebook onto the desk. "For three hundred dollars we could drive to Paris."

I put down the bottle and turned to look at Thor. Somewhere over our rooftop, I was confident, the clouds had parted and on shafts of golden light some heavenly choir caroled to earth onc single, glorious word: "Paris!" The word was music itself. Salvation was at hand. How could we have been so dense?

I poured the drinks and slipped into the chair beside Thor. "You are a dear and brilliant man," I said. I put my arm through his. "However, we can discuss that at length over a glass of Beaujolais on the Champs-Elysées. That's where all the cafés are, isn't it?"

Thor lifted his chin from his hand and stared at me. "What are you talking about?"

Images of Paris flipped through my brain: sidewalk cafés, and the Seine, and Gene Kelly tapping through sunlit streets to the warm laughter of French children. "Thor," I said. "Listen to me. How much is the deposit on the car?"

"Shipping deposit?"

"Shipping."

"Two hundred dollars."

"Maybe they'll give it back. Or maybe they'll let us ship it out of Calais or Marseilles or someplace and apply the deposit. We can ask."

"What in God's name are you talking about?"

"Driving to Paris."

"Driving to Paris!" he cried. "We haven't got enough money to wait it out where we are, and you want to drive to Paris."

"We take the luggage that we were going to ship *inside* the car and put it *on top of* the car. On the car rack," I said. "There'll be room for the four of us in the VW."

It was all falling into place in my mind. "We'll have a lot better time than we would in two weeks in a Copenhagen hotel room. We'll see Europe, Thor."

Europe, I thought, not just a tiny island in the Baltic. "I'll bet we can do it for less than it would cost us to wait it out here."

Thor wasn't frowning anymore. "Paris," he said. "Paris in the spring."

"Right!" I said. "We drive to Paris and walk into that bank and cash that stupid draft ourselves. It doesn't take two weeks to get to Paris does it?"

"Three or four days. Less. We could do it in three and still see a lot of country." His brain was fully functioning again. I knew what was going through it. "Sarah," he began.

"Sarah's asleep as soon as the car rolls."

"Katie," he said. "It would be a great experience for Katie."

"A great experience."

Thor had traveled in Western Europe. He would enjoy playing guide.

But then his smile drooped. "We can't do it," he groaned. "That damn draft is en route somewhere. We're going to wind up waiting for that damn draft."

"Not so!" I said, and told him about the telegram.

He began walking around. I gave him his drink.

"How much cash have we actually got?"

"Two hundred and forty-five U.S. dollars and more than a hundred in kroner."

He walked over to the desk. "Are all the maps packed away?"

"I put them all in the glove compartment of the car."

He stared out the window. "What about those luggage straps?"

"Also in the car."

"I can make some kind of permanent support for Sarah's basket in the back seat. Make as much room as possible for Katie." He walked to the window and stared at the car. "I think all the luggage can go on the roof. We'll have to ship the scooter." And he rubbed his chin.

I waited.

"We can get our overnight stuff under the hood," he said.

"Well, you know best."

"And we'll keep quiet about our plans."

"Right," I said. "Keep it quiet."

"No sense getting everybody stirred up."

"No sense."

"Paris," he said.

I threw my arms around his neck.

"Oh Thor! We can, can't we, really fly home from Paris?"

He put his arms around me.

"I don't know why not," he said. "Trust me!"

Getting back our shipping deposit on the car was no problem. Apparently people were lined up waiting for shipping space.

We decided after all to tell Tove of our change of plans. It had become awkward dissuading her from seeing us off in Copenhagen. And suddenly the need to keep our plans from any of the villagers seemed absurd.

They took it casually. Americans were given to unpredictable behavior. So it was Paris, was it? They had long suspected we were quite wealthy, simply given to an odd life style.

The night before we left we had a farewell drink at the pilot's house together with our "touching neighbors"—those whose property surrounded ours. The villagers' farewells to the children were devastating and interminable, and on the morning of our departure, we sent Katie off to Franz's so that she would not be wrenched from our departing car by tearful neighbors. Franz's mother had arranged a goodbye brunch for the two of them.

As the hour of leaving approached, Tove brought Thor and me a bag of doughnuts "for our journey." It was dreadful leaving her. She would not stay and watch us drive away.

Our car was packed. We stood on the street. I needed to make one final check of the house. A truck with a Copenhagen logo on it drove up and two workmen got out. "They're early," I said to Thor. Technically we had another full day before the onslaught of the cottage's remodeling team.

One of the men made their apologies. "Just wanted to see what we're in for," he said, "and we'll be on our way."

I went back into the open house and the two men followed. They clumped across the living room, an alien presence in our gentle cottage.

"First thing is to get this ladder out of here," the head man said, standing in the kitchen, looking up to the second floor. He kicked the bottom rung, and the ladder groaned.

"Hey, take a look at this," his companion called. He was standing over the *kakkolovn*. His boss joined him. Together they stared at the venerable iron stove. "Another death trap," the workman said. "No proper vent. We'll have to knock out some wall space for a panel ray."

The boss looked at me.

"Are all the bedrooms upstairs?"

"The bedroom is upstairs," I said.

The older man jerked his thumb toward the ceiling, sending the younger one back into the kitchen and up the offending ladder. After a minute the man yelled from above. "Hey, you gotta see this!"

The older man moved into the kitchen and peered upward. "What?" he yelled.

"Old-time beds," came the voice. "Three of them. Set in the wall. All in one room."

There was a pause. His companion had no intention of climbing the ladder. "If we pull them out, can we get two rooms out of it up there?"

There was another pause.

"Small ones."

I picked up the duffel bag with Sarah's diapers and went out to the cobblestone street. Thor had finished arranging the back seat, and Sarah was propped up in the basket.

"What's the matter?" he said when he saw me.

"They're going to tear the place up," I said. Through the window I could see the workmen in their soiled white uniforms plunging around like dirty polar bears in a dollhouse. Thor put his arms around me.

We waited until the men had gotten into their truck and left, and then we went back into the house.

There was a barrette of Katie's on a table, and I put it in my pocket. Thor went up the ladder and I heard him gently close the doors on the beds. He came down and we stood in the little kitchen with its window facing the sound and under it the single faucet dripping an occasional dollup of water into the dark, zink-lined sink. I reached out and squeezed the tap until the dripping stopped.

At the front door I turned for a final image of the place, something I could hold in my mind, forever frozen in time. And then Thor came back and moved me out through the garden and onto the street.

We had said all our good-byes. I was glad. I could not have said one word.

We got into the car. A hundred yards away a pilot boat was tacking its way into the harbor, wind filling the red-striped sail. We drove along beside the sea, past the school and the church and on to Franz's house. The VW rolled along. I could see the shadows of our luggage rack reflected in the windows of familiar houses.

"By now Katie will have figured out a way to strap Franz on top," Thor said. "How are you on early betrothals?"

"No," I said, finding my voice. "I think Katie will negotiate an eventual trip for Franz to the United States. She's been working on his father for a month.''

"And me for two," Thor said.

We got out to say our good-byes to Franz and his family. Katie was voluble. ''And remember what I told you,'' she said, at last moving toward the car, and looking archly at Franz. Franz's mother stood in the doorway waving.

I wanted to ruffle Franz's blond hair with my hand and give him a hug. But it was clearly hand-shaking time, and we all got through it with the proper combination of eye-locking intimacy and formal head bowing. ''I do hope you can come see us, Franz.''

Katie put her hand on my arm.

"Don't worry Mom," she said, and then: ''See you Franz. Take care of things here.''

"I will," he said. ''See you, Katie.''

And we three got in the car, and with Sarah we left Taarnby.

Epilogue

My account of our year of fieldwork in Taarnby was sporadic in its reporting, focused perhaps too much on the misadventures (mine) rather than on the small victories and progressive insights that are often hard won in anthropological research.

For many students, first fieldwork is being done today with fewer problems than marked my debut. Many graduate departments offer courses in field methods and research strategies. A few have pioneered in the introduction of advanced seminars that make use of computer technologies in the gathering and processing of field data.

In the numbers of field-experienced anthropologists and in the proliferation of anthropology faculties, students have more role models. When I was a graduate student, there were few women to emulate. Margaret Mead, Cora DuBois, and Ruth Benedict were among the principal luminaries; glimpses of what life was like in the field filtered through the pages of their widely read books. But the mechanics of day-to-day, month-to-month productivity in the field remained, for the most part, an elusive insight.

The all-male faculty to which I was subject tried to avoid prejudicial postures about women in the field and largely succeeded, although the first faculty member I met, an acting chairman, told me that archaeology was no specialty for me and I shouldn't think about going into it. I did not disagree with him. Archaeology struck me as a tedious business. I had no desire to carve out a career in it. I ignored his next suggestion, that I enroll at another university. An East Coast women's university was recommended by name.

The bearded young men with pipes who dominated the advanced graduate group looked as though they had entered the world with boots on. There was no way I could emulate them even if I had wanted to. Under the rubric of good clean fun, teasing and a kind of ritualized defamation of character were widespread. I was not particularly singled out for it. Nor was

I exempted. When I got the only A in an otherwise all male seminar on fictive kinship, my five classmates had ready a suggestion as to how I might have favorably influenced my grade. And when I almost flunked a linguistics midterm, questions about the genetic predisposition of the female brain in areas of hard science became a subject for audible discussion. On the other hand, one of these same male students volunteered the time to unravel for me the mystery of fricatives and sibilants until I had committed to memory enough linguistics to get through the Language and Culture final with a B.

In the field, being a woman brought advantages and disadvantages. In the maritime community of Taarnby, Denmark, doors were less frequently open to me than they were to Thor. Given Thor's language proficiency, the villagers understandably were more comfortable with him from the start. He, too, experienced limitations in adapting to particular person-to-person scenarios. We didn't keep score. Thor treated me as a fellow professional though I was without the doctorate. Never were we particularly absorbed with whatever sex-linked impediments to the research may have been operating. Our priority was to get the job done. For the most part, each of us moved most freely in whatever household we had—in some way—initiated contact. The luck of the draw.

We experienced more advantages than disadvantages as a family in the field, and in having added to that family. In the face of our professional ambiguity (never resolved), villagers were comforted in our husband/wife, father/mother roles. Less suspicion attached to us.

I wish we had studies of the long-term effects of fieldwork on the children of anthropologists. From time to time in Taarnby we worried about Katie. I would think: God! we've disrupted her education, plunged her into a language she will probably never again have use for, and created heaven knows what psychic garbage that will surface in the years to come. Later years discounted my worries. Katie herself values the experience. Sarah could not have had more attention or caring stimulation.

Wherever and however it is done—with or without spouse and children—fieldwork is characterized by more fluid boundaries between personal life and work life than exist in the home environment of the anthropologist. As we reached out for involvement in the daily life of the families of Taarnby, all aspects of our lives became areas of appropriate, and sometimes avid, interest for them. When in that first week, I drove Thor and Katie and me out of our smoke-filled house into the visibility of Taarnby's cobbled streets, I launched (more precipitously than necessary) our joint exploration of one another's worlds. The next twelve months were a dynamic extension of that encounter, with incalculable dividends (and frustrations) for all involved.

In professional terms, our year in Taarnby yielded a book, several articles, and considerable lecture mileage.

Today when I am in the field, I record the unpublished side of fieldwork in a journal, separate from my field notes. I track my impressions of persons and events, large and small, which absorb or confuse, delight or frighten me in the daily course of work—wherever I find myself. In these pages accumulate my reactions to the painstaking overtures to involvement in local life, the small achievements and numerous things gone wrong (in whose genesis I seem to remain influential), the building of friendships (and sometimes animosities). In brief, the struggle to identify and appreciate different worlds, and—importantly for me—my changing self as anthropologist.

Compelling always is the travail of coming to terms with dependency on the local community, of acquiring some mastery of the language that brings order and meaning to a particular way of life, so different from one's own.

Fieldwork lies at the foundation of anthropology. Without protracted periods in the field, the understanding of culture— anthropology's domain—is enfeebled into vicarious speculation. Without the experience of fieldwork, students pursue a more imperfect and troublesome course in their development as anthropologists.

Foreign fieldwork is a personal as well as a professional crucible; perhaps it has to be, for more than any other discipline, anthropology has its roots in the appreciation of values: how and along what lines cultures establish and prize the priorities that shape their worlds. Those of us who regard the examination of these value systems as a worthy science need to understand the boundaries of relativity that shape our own. The field, in worlds where our homegrown values do not obtain and in which we must live at length, is the only place to do that.

In the field we ask inevitably not only "Who are they?" but also "Who am I?"—here bereft of old reassurances of identity and self-worth. The recurrent challenge to find answers, in some way to laminate the private and professional domains of self, is a continuing dimension of life as an anthropologist.

The yearlong field experience allows the embryonic anthropologist time to explore and accept the obligations and dividends of professionalism. There is time and stimulus enough to foster security in what we do and pride in what we are. Progress toward these goals is at best uneven. If it is achieved, however, the product is sustained personal and professional growth.

I would rather be an anthropologist than anything in the world (except perhaps a prima ballerina). Twenty-five years after Taarnby, each new field experience brings with it that same strange mixture of exhilaration and palm-moistening apprehension I knew when launched into that first of many unpredictable worlds. Some of us gradually get better at exploring them. Most of us become addicted to the sheer adventure of it.

✦❁◉❀❁✦

One of the grant proposals that I had submitted from Taarnby paid off. In Paris we communicated to Tove the news of our safe arrival, and learned of a cable that had come after our departure. The National Science Foundation awarded us financial support to replicate, in a French village, our Danish study of the impact of creeping urbanization on traditional life styles.

It would be two more years before we returned to the United States—by then a family of *five*. Our son, Thomas, was born a French villager.

✦❁◉❀❁✦